Enchanting Whiskers - A Photobook

Captivating Moments with Curious Kittens

By Photopydia

"Just watching my cats can make me happy." – Paula Cole.

"Cats are connoisseurs of comfort." – James Herriot.

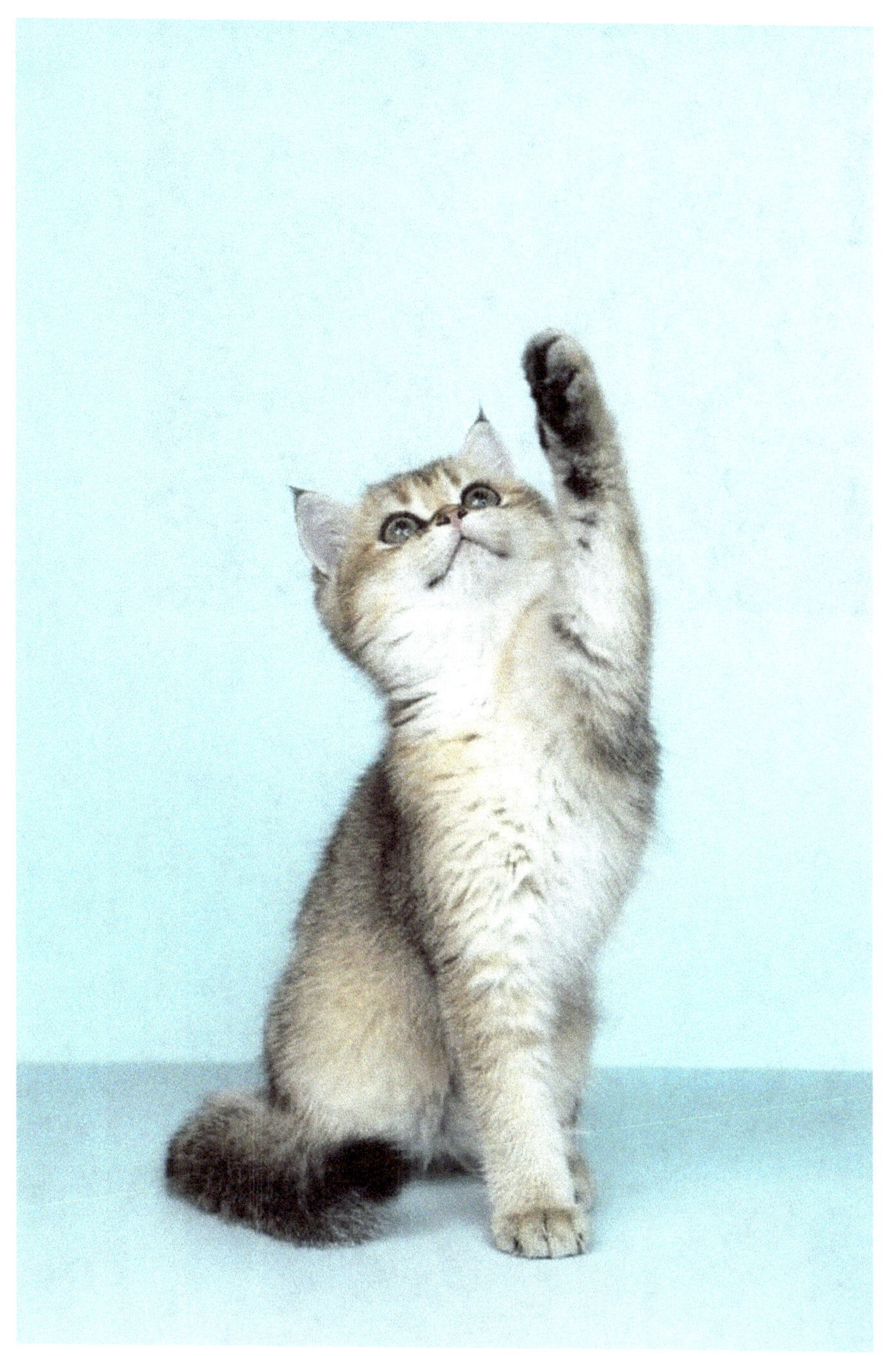

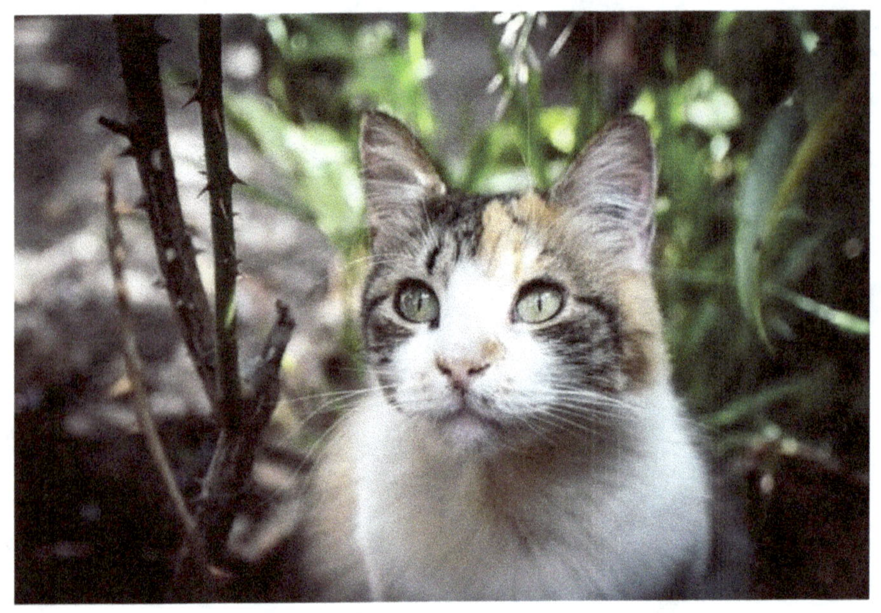

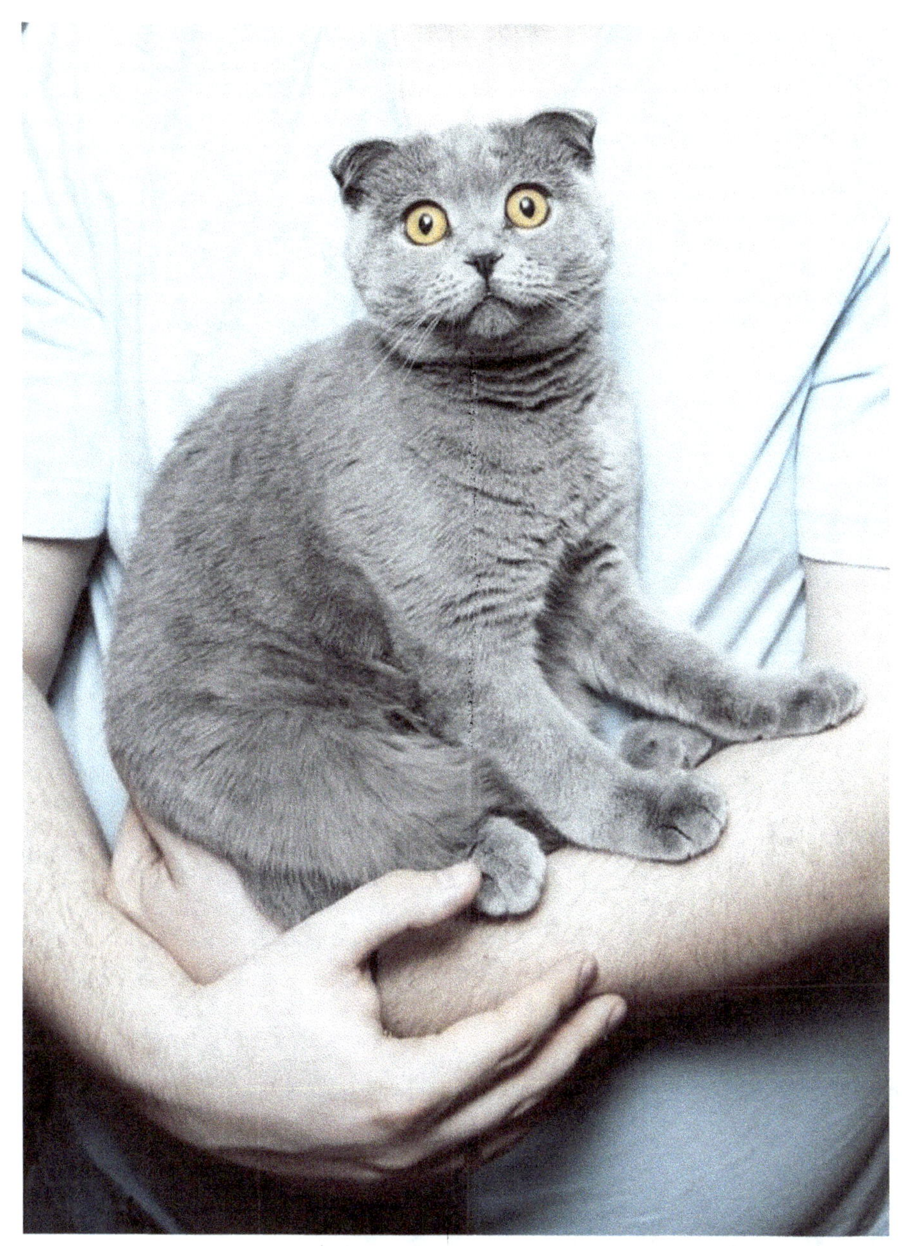

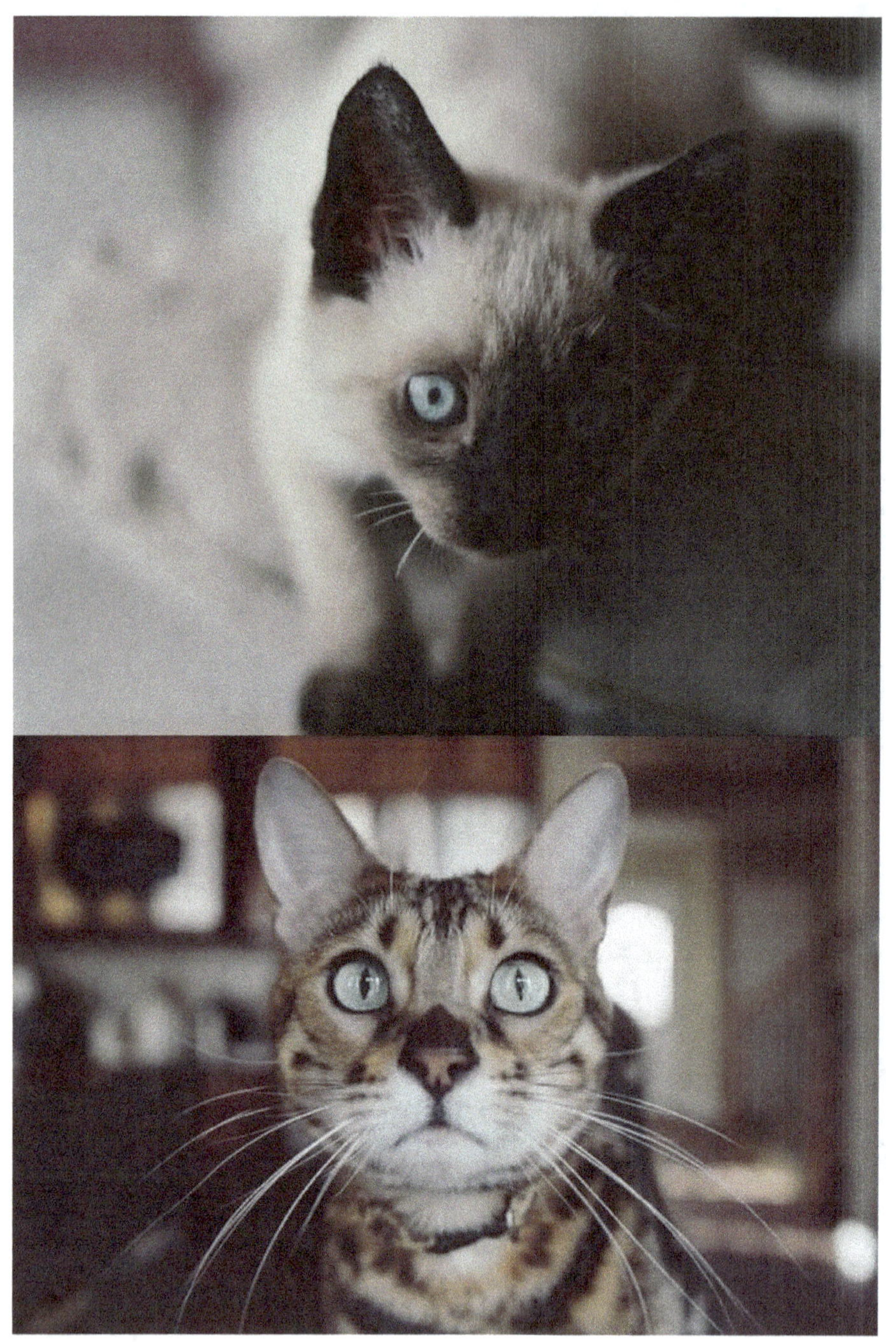

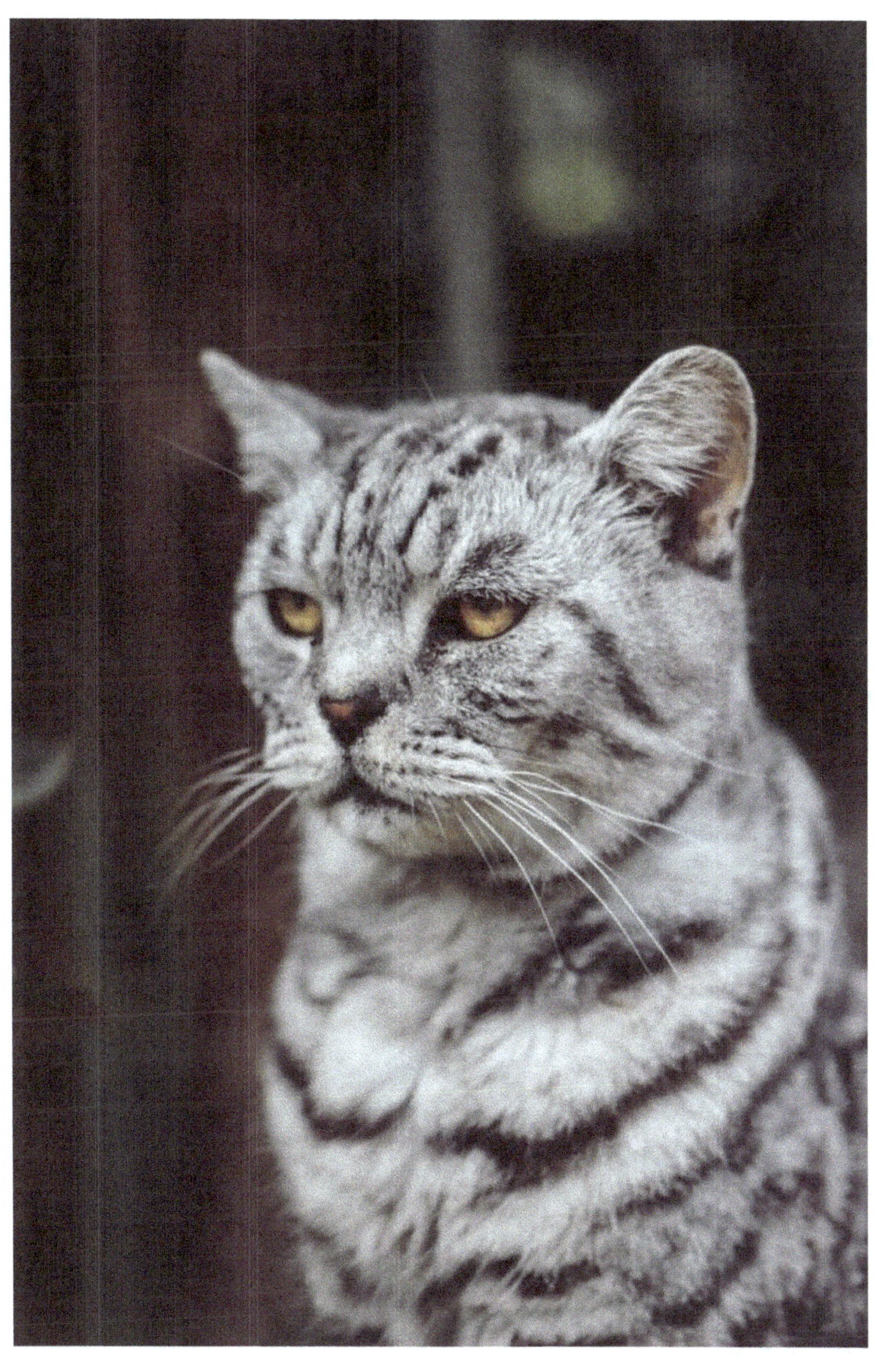

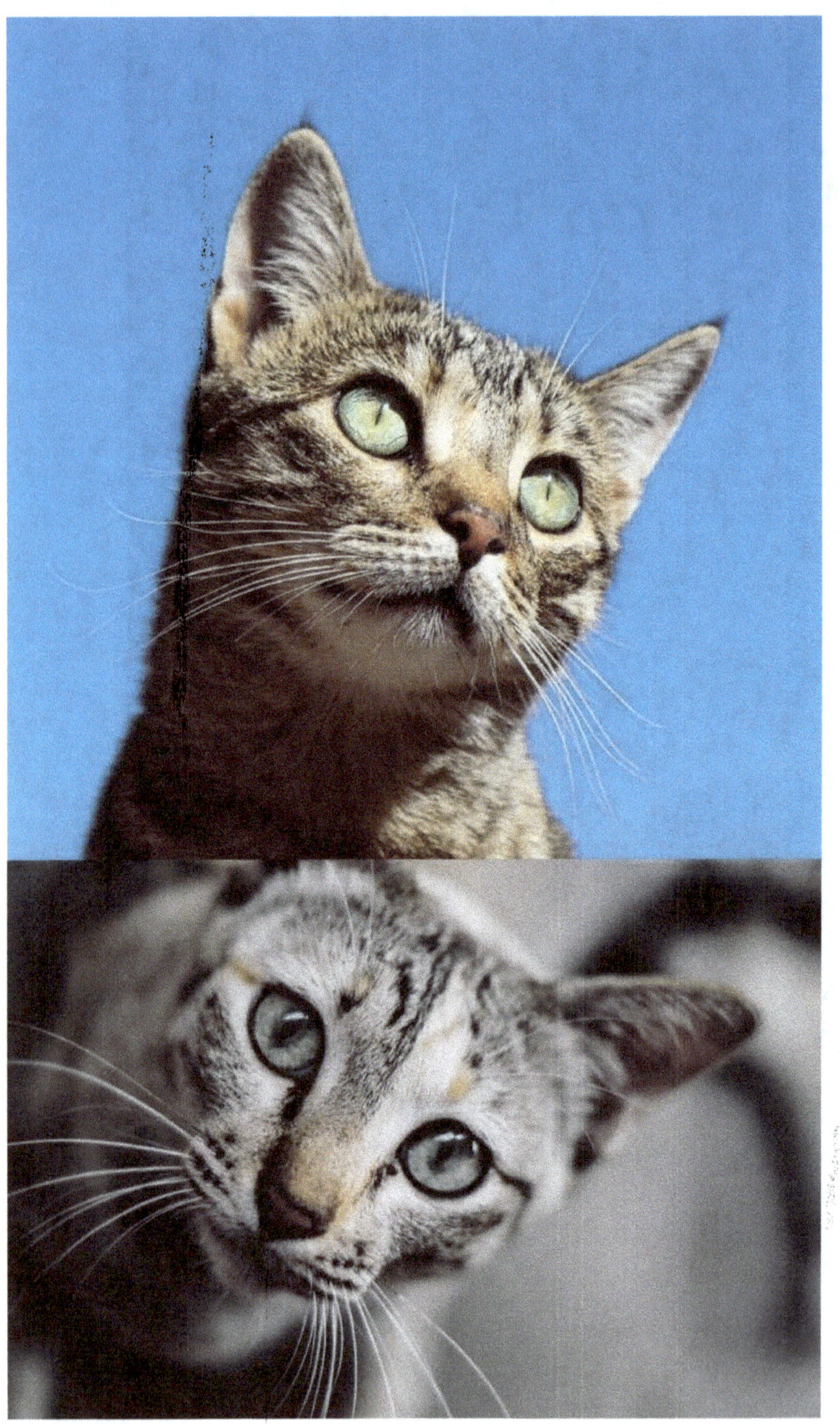

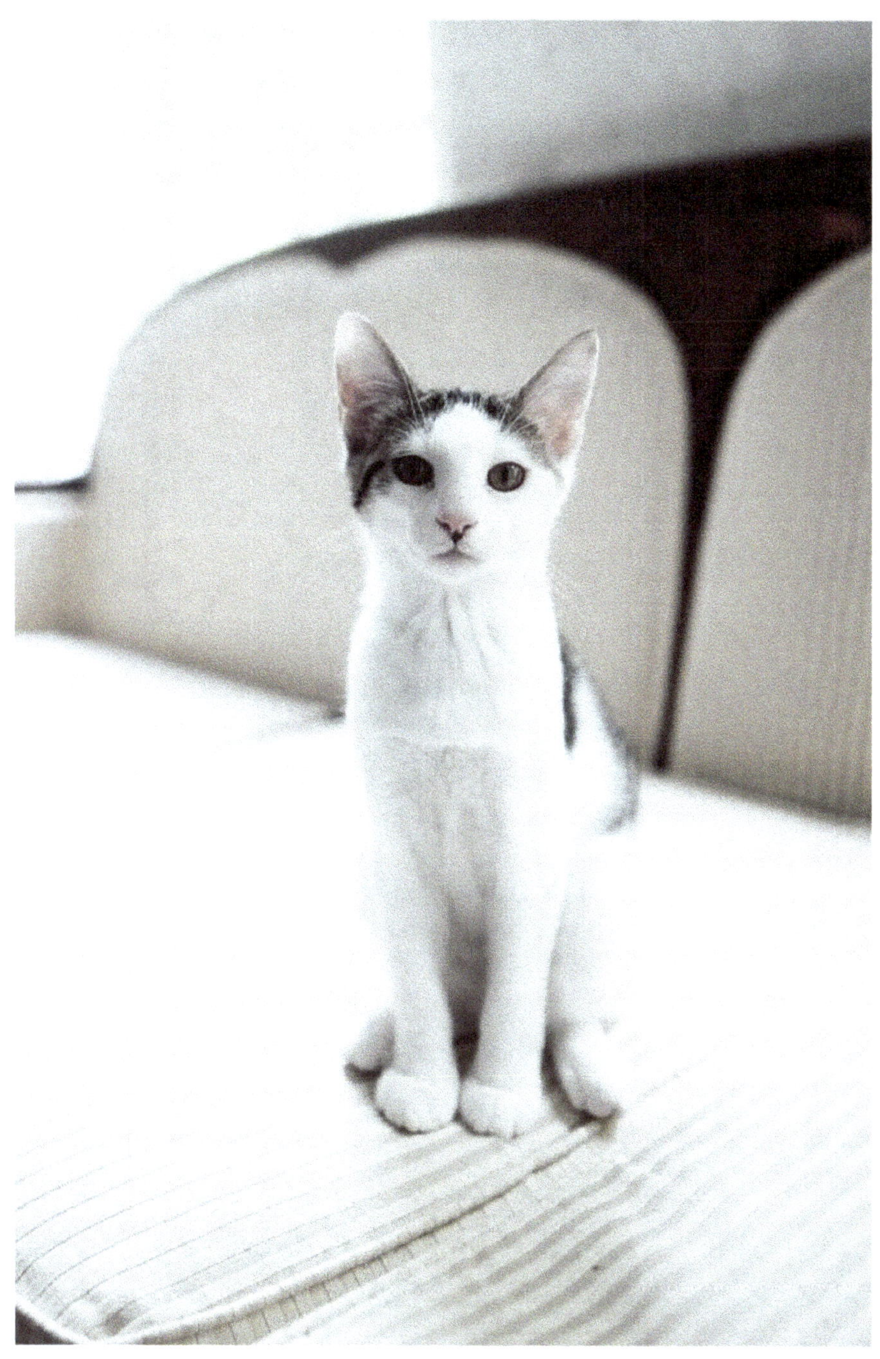

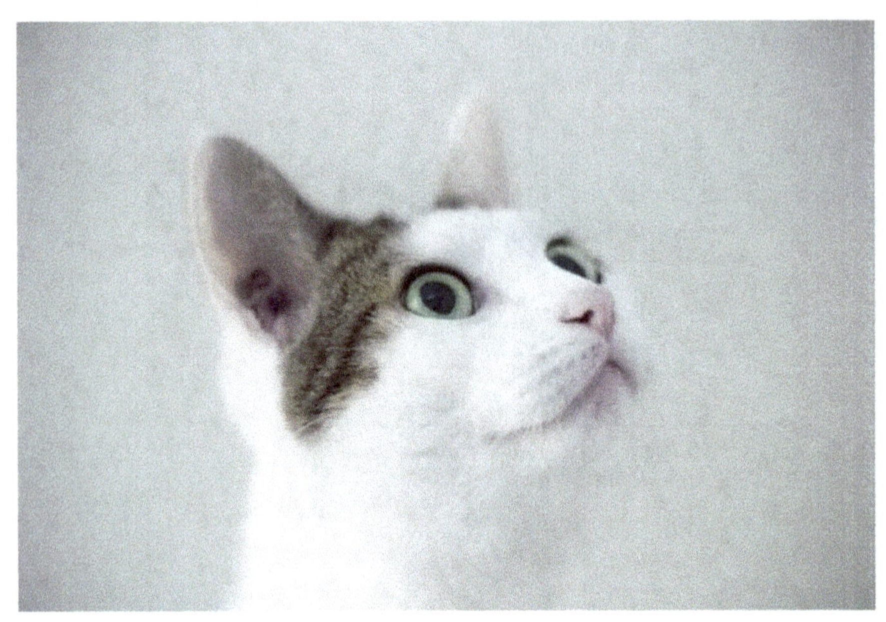

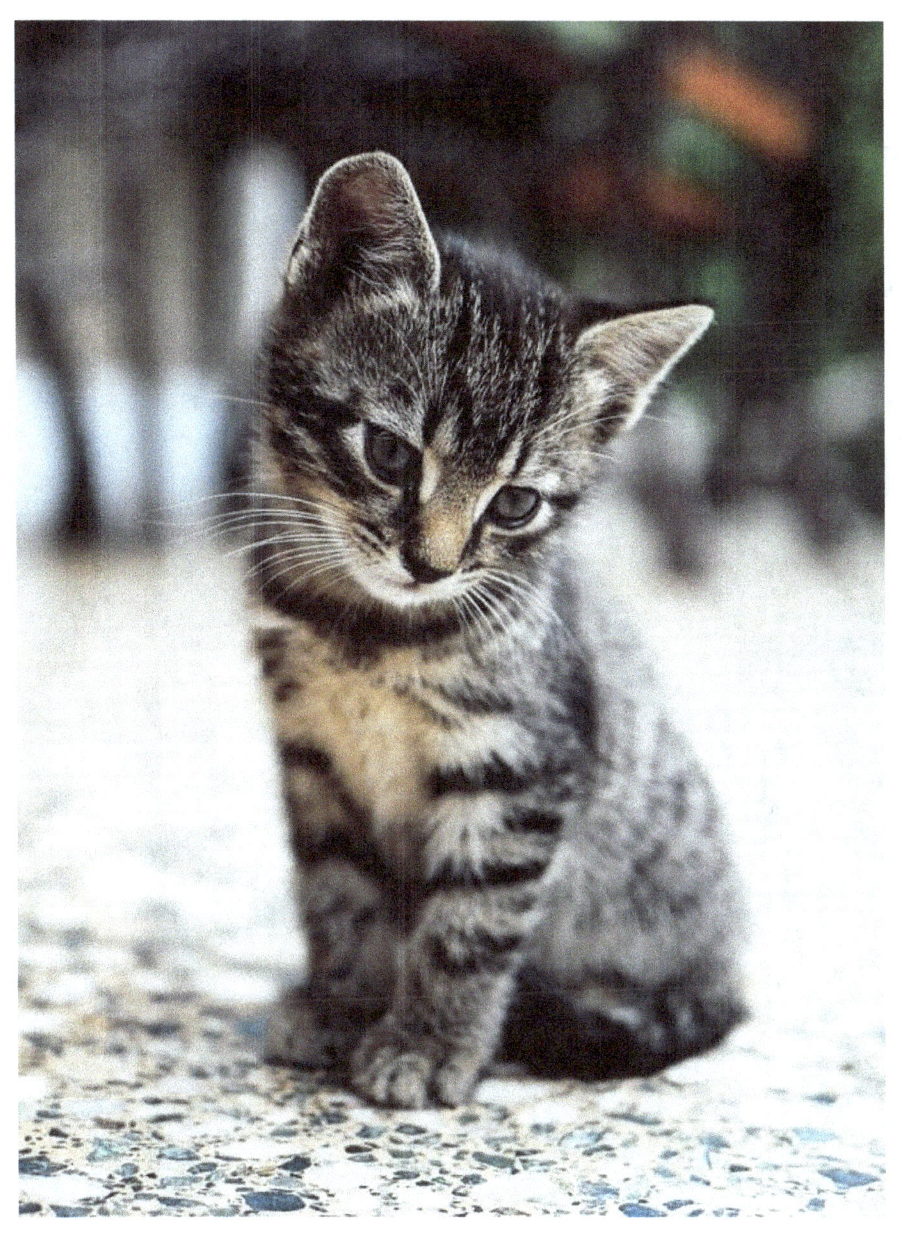

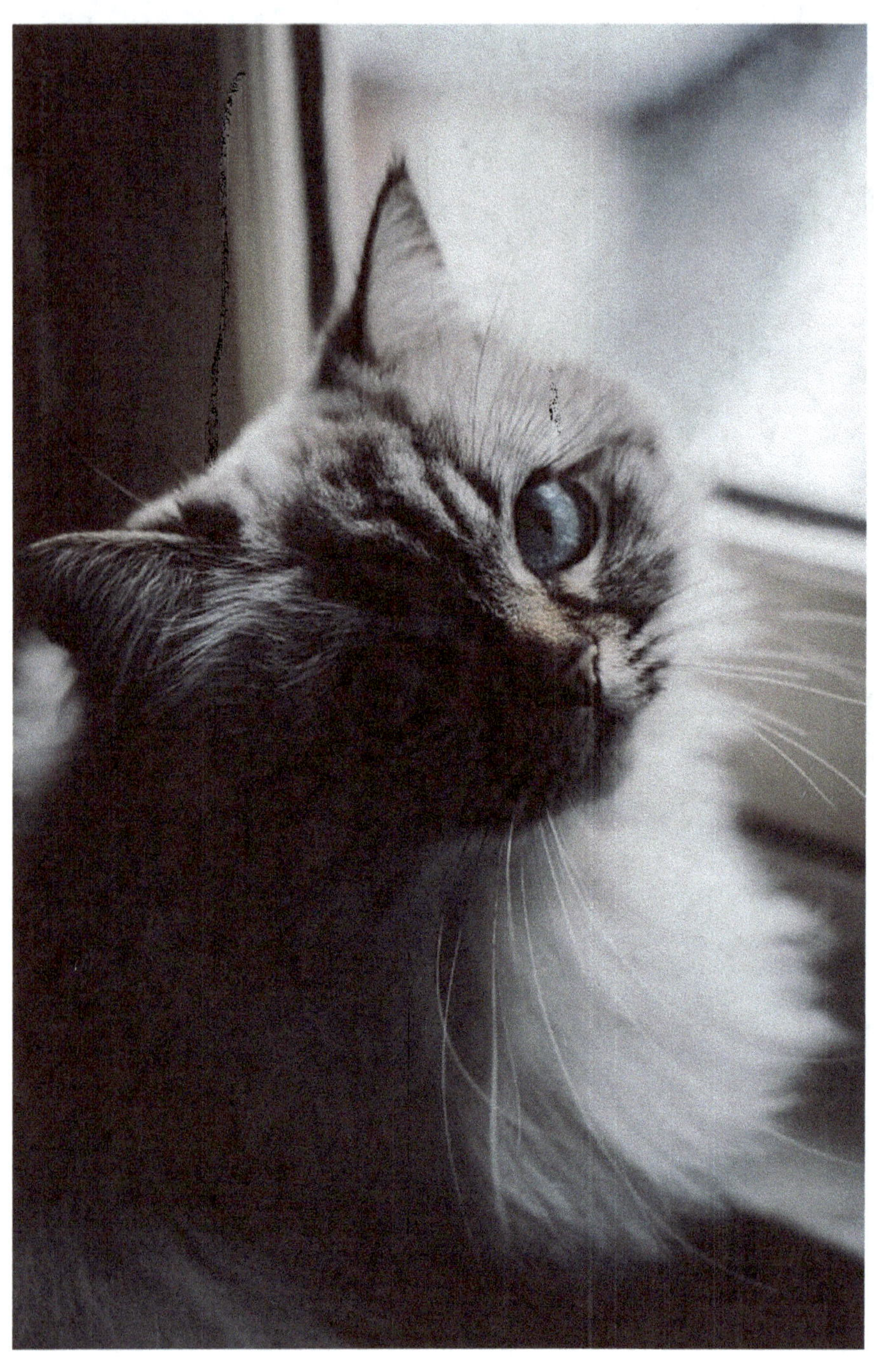

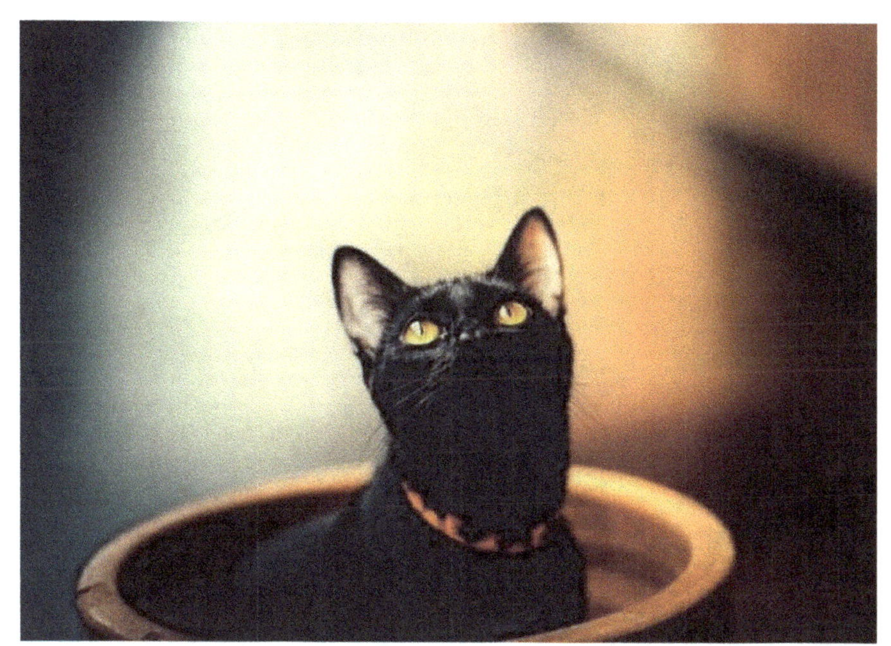

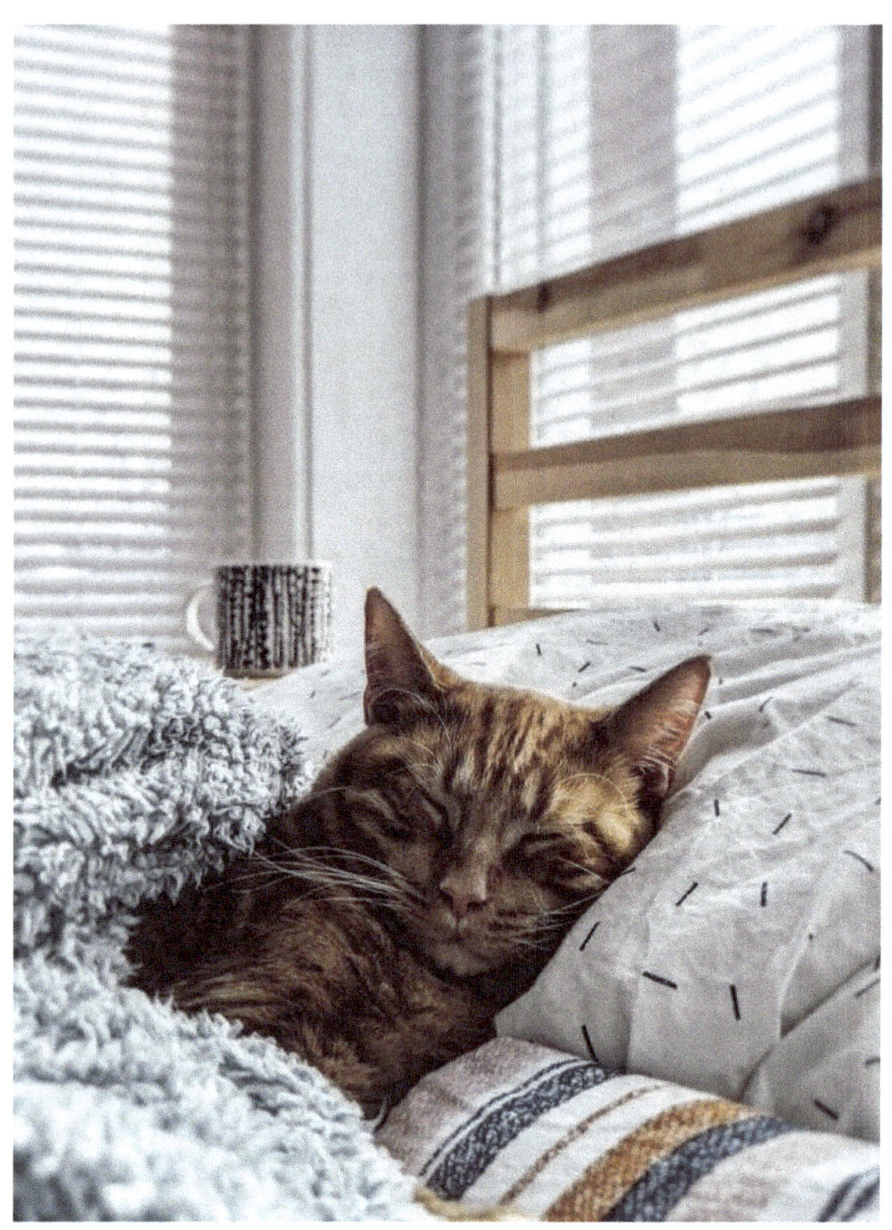

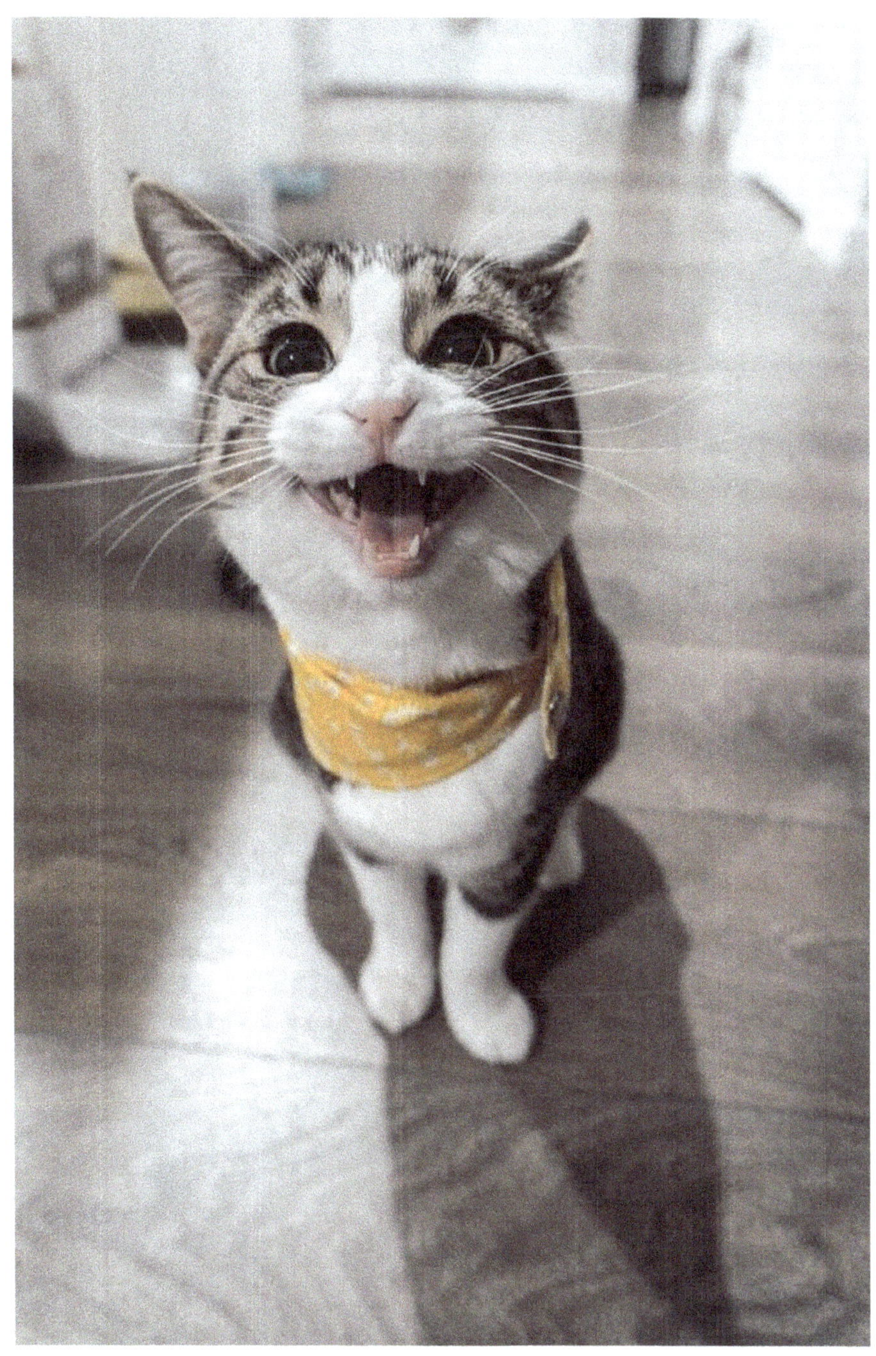

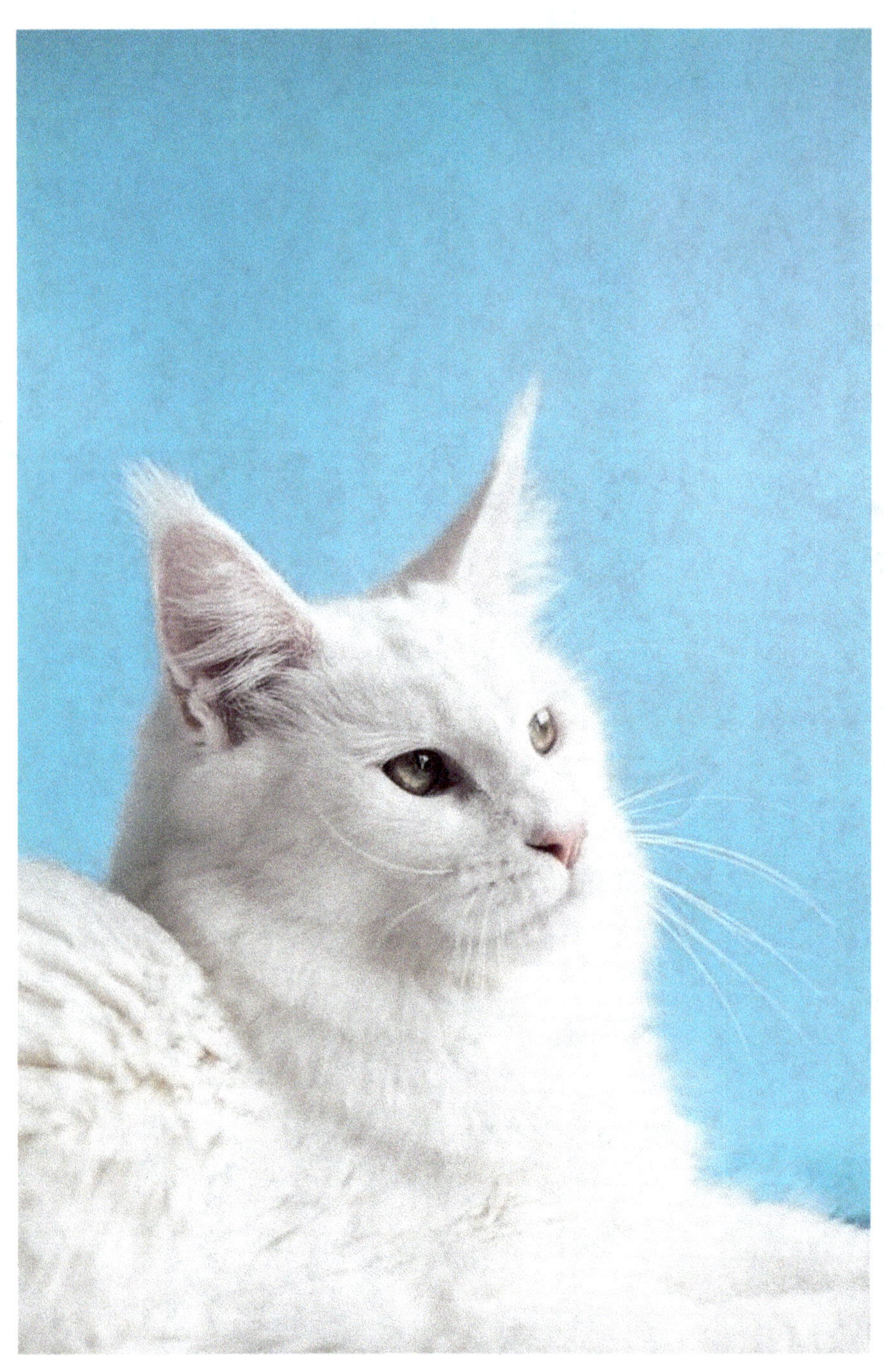

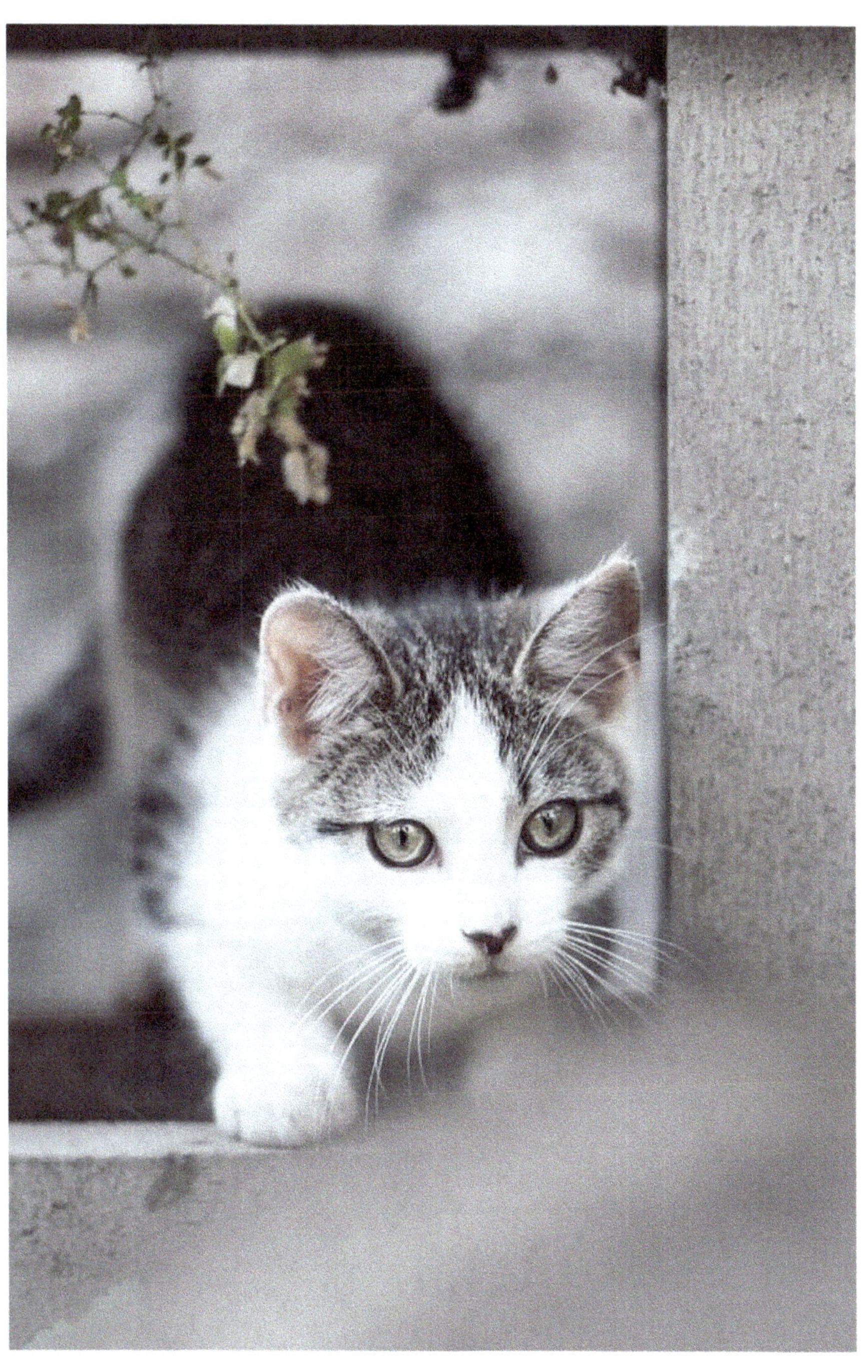

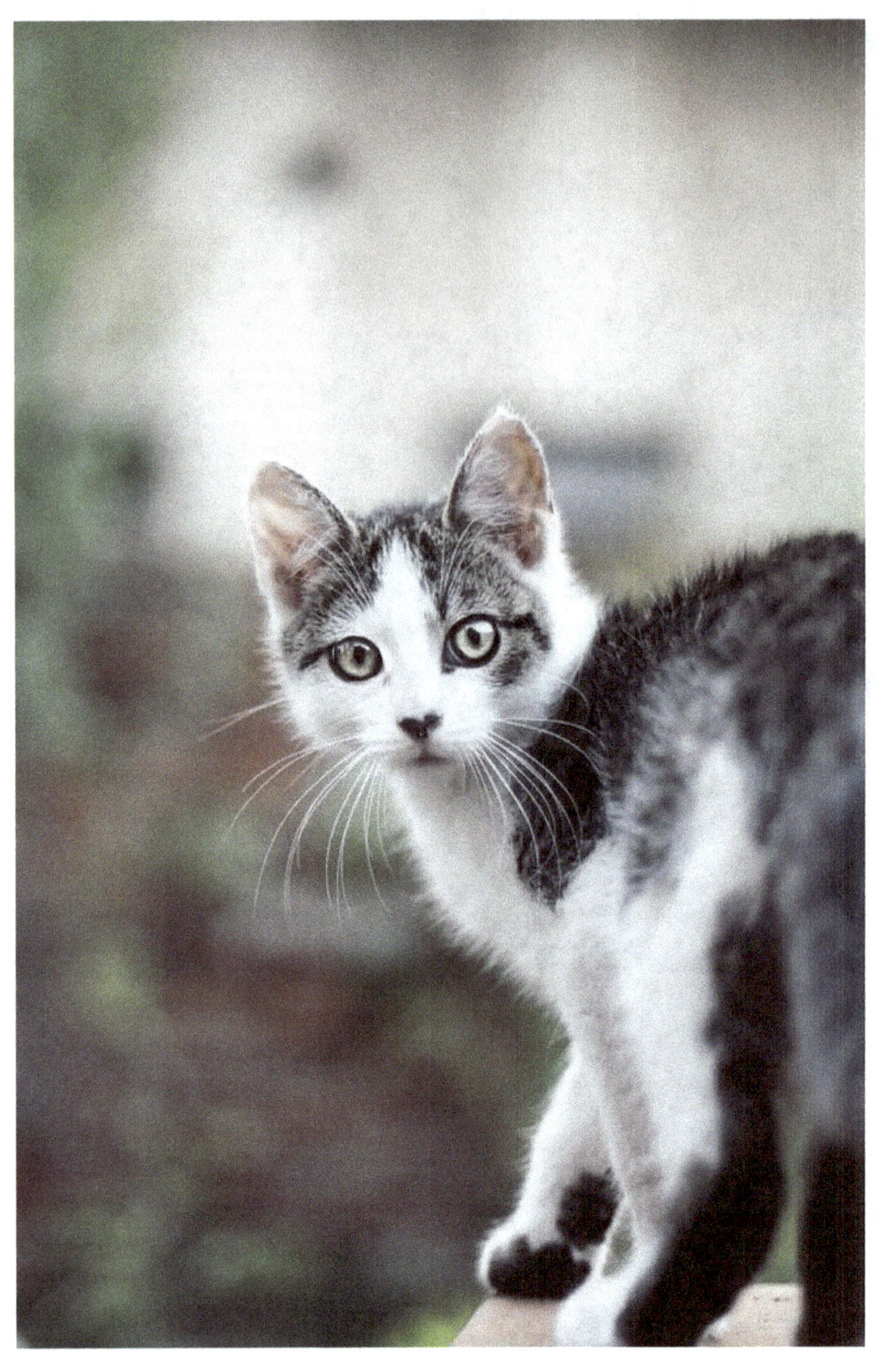

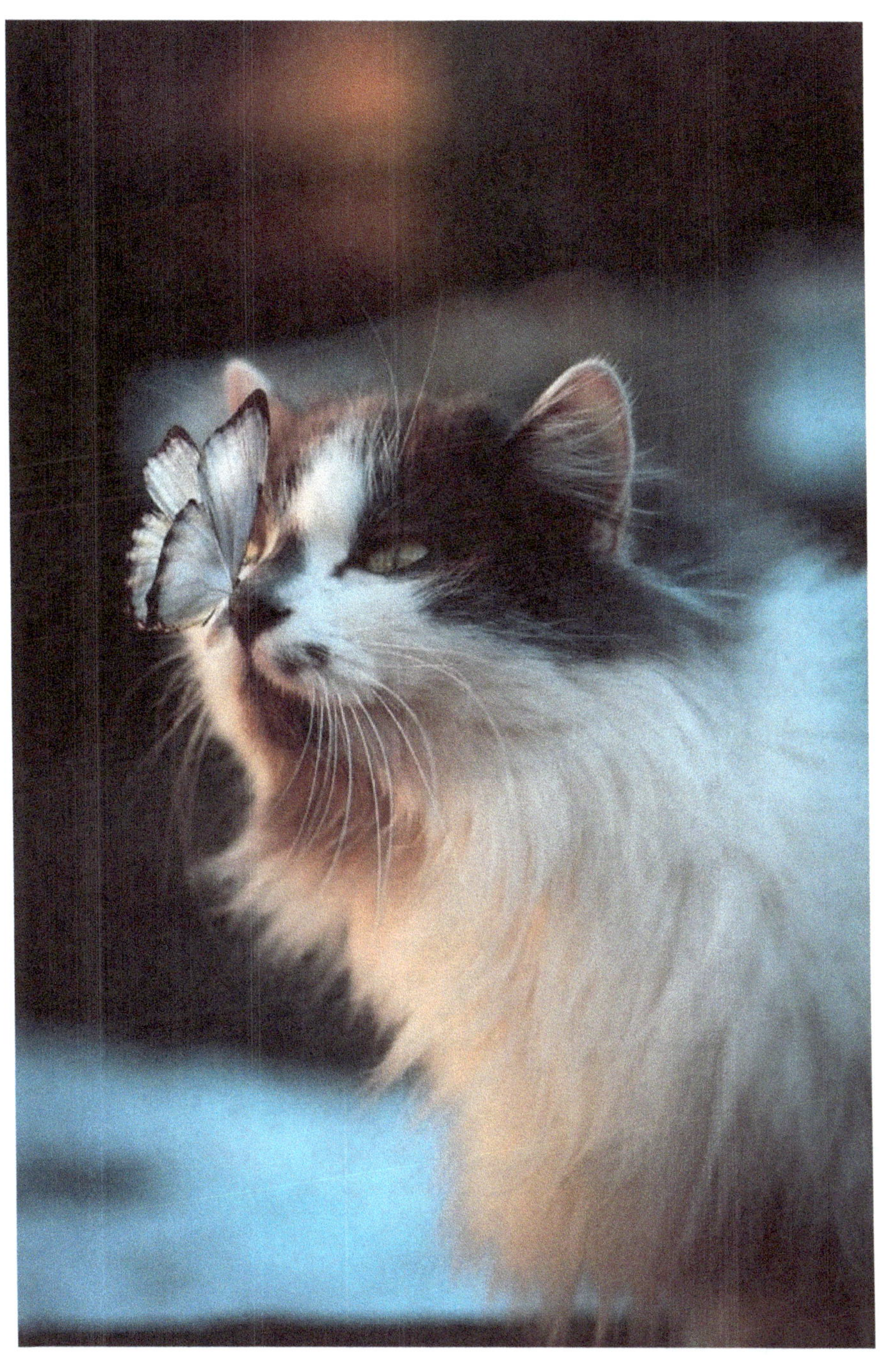

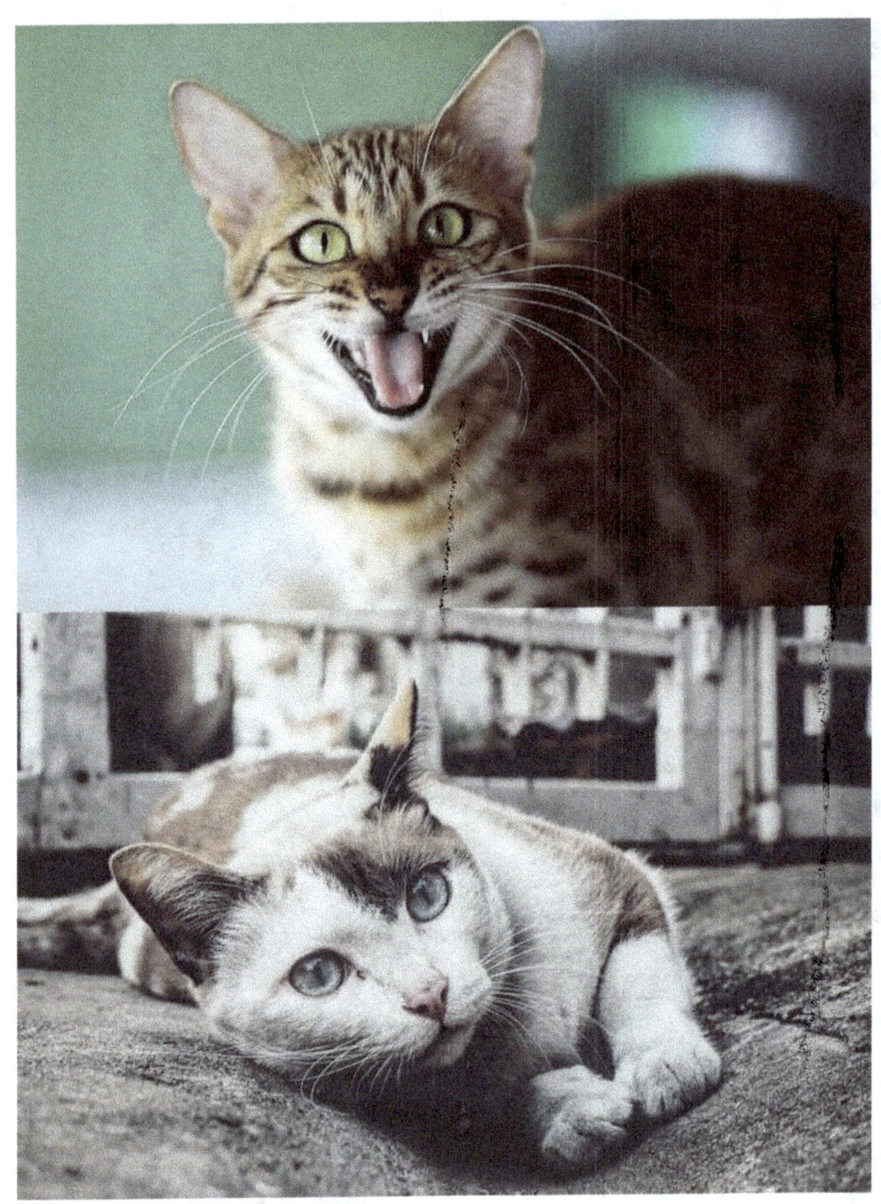

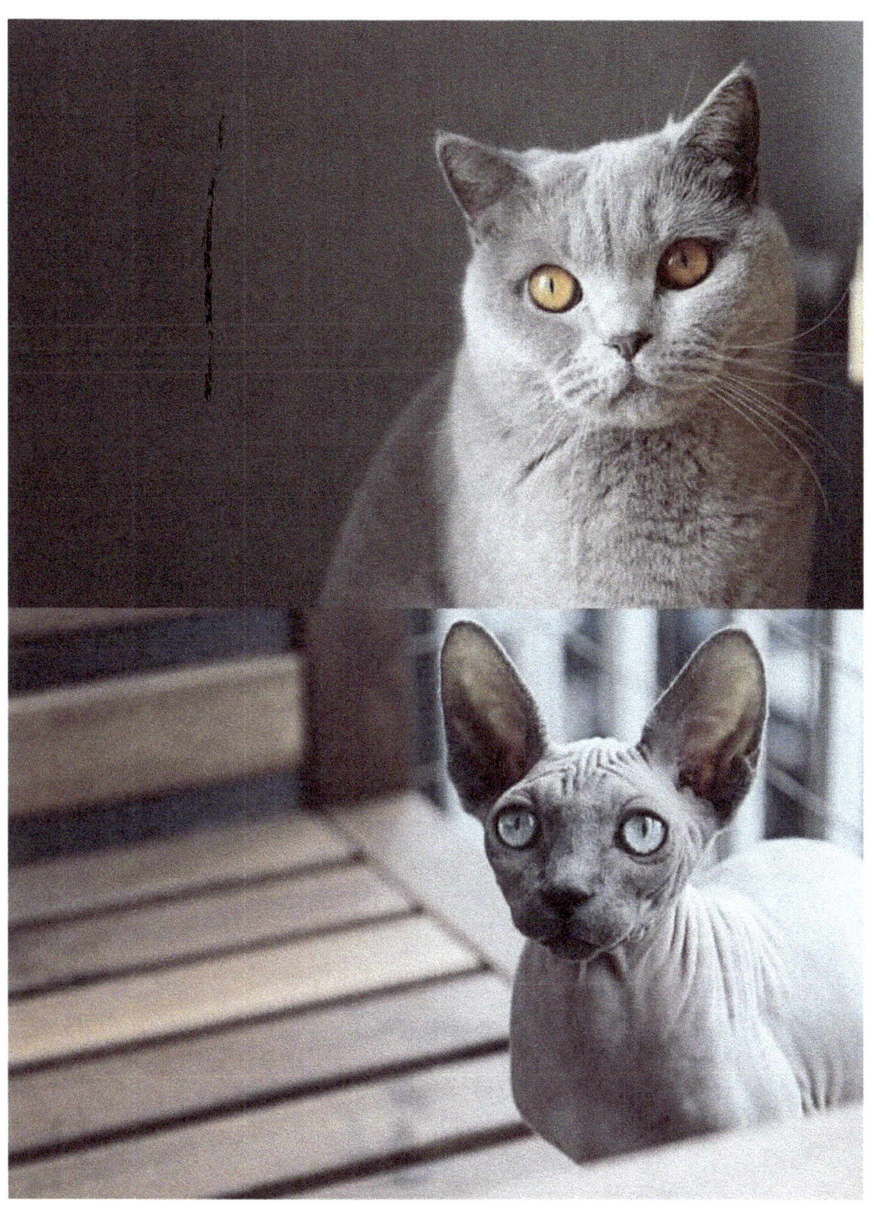

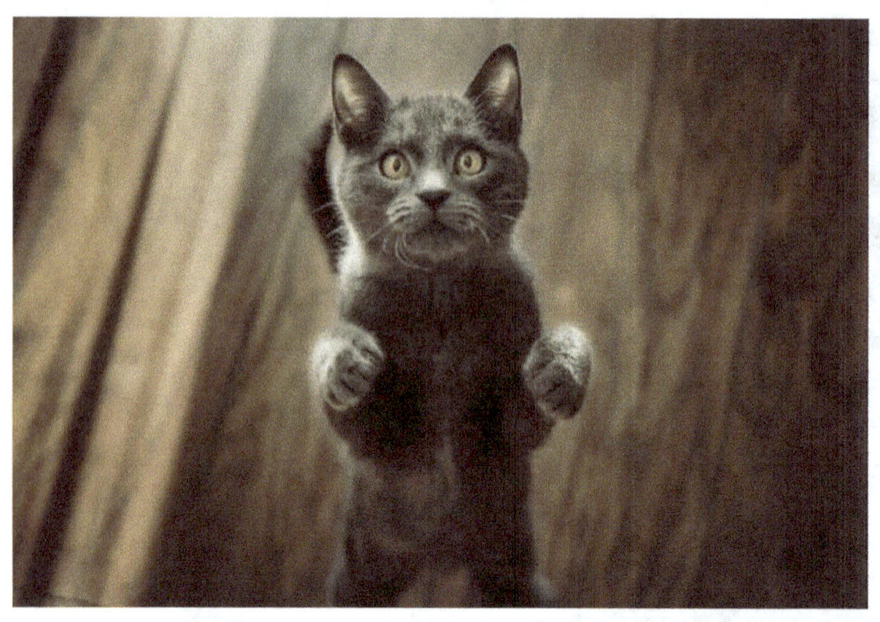

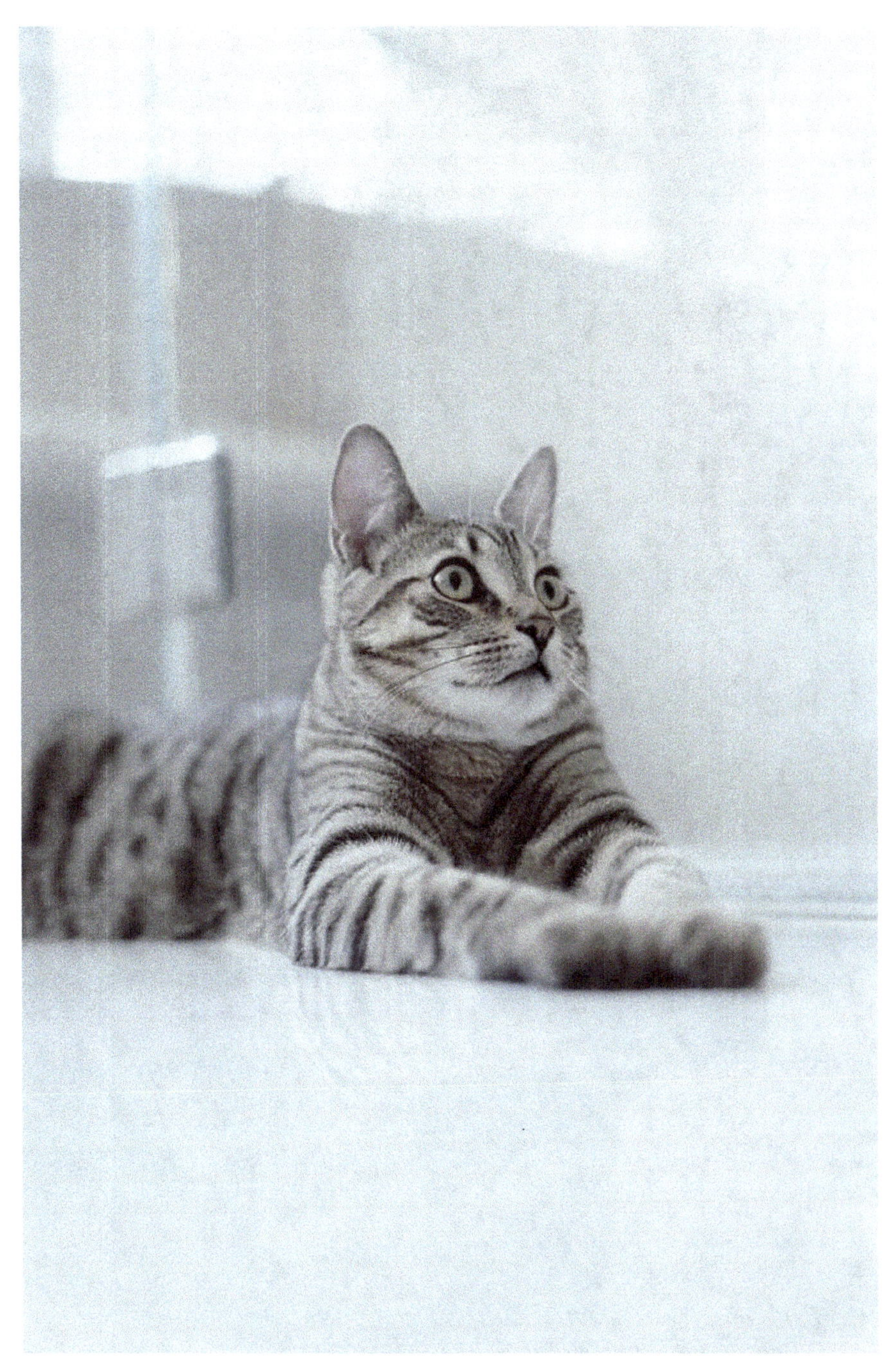

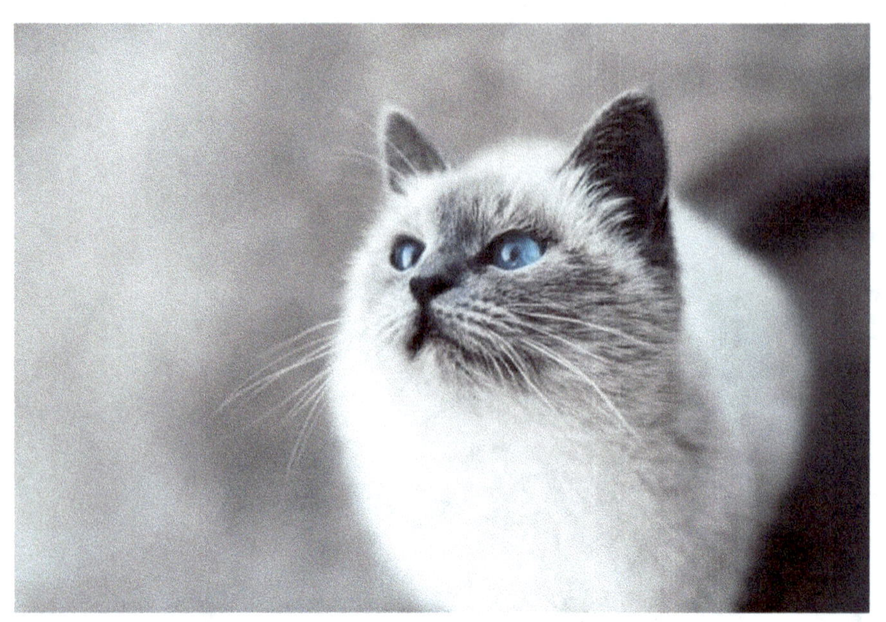

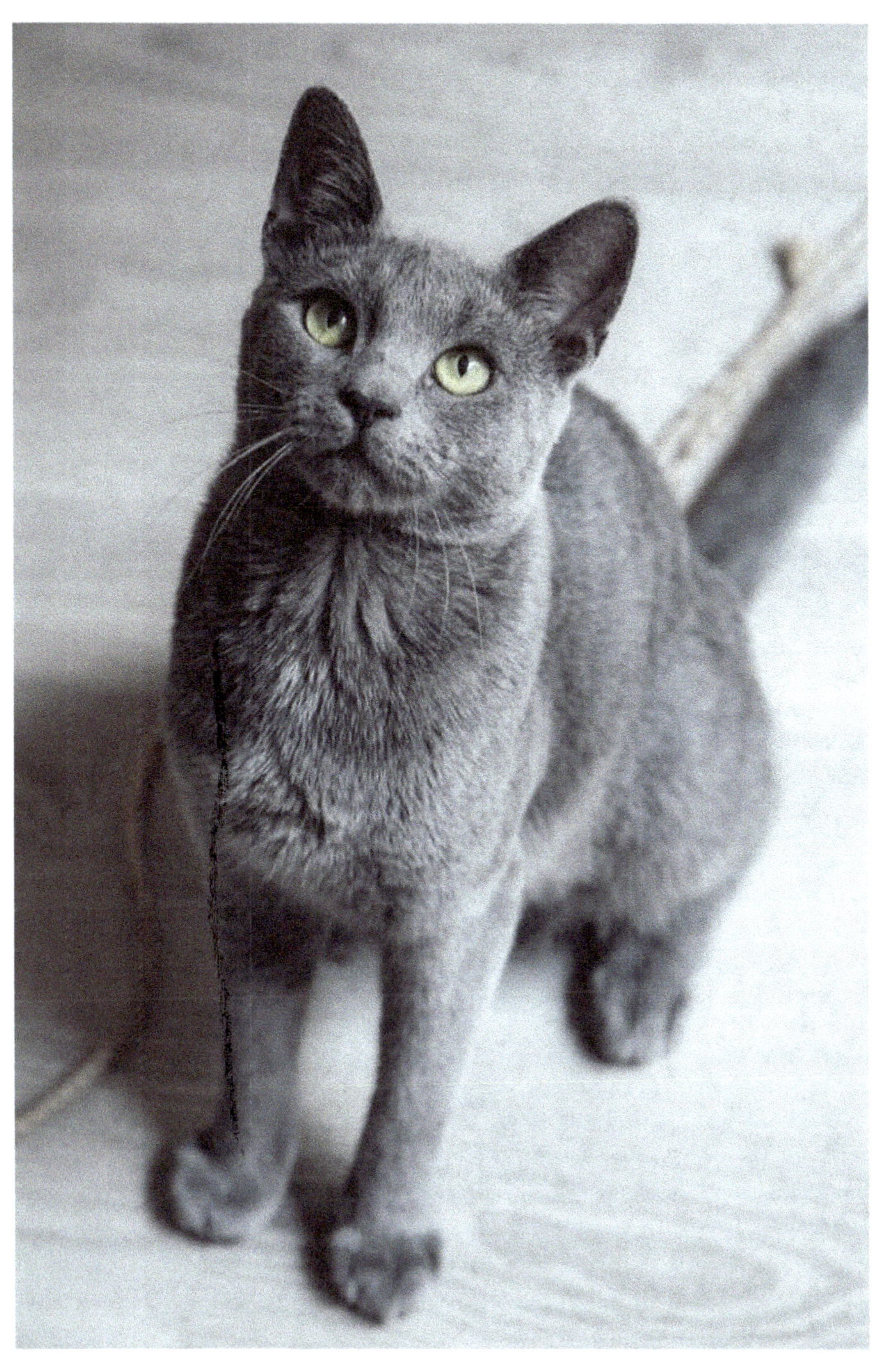

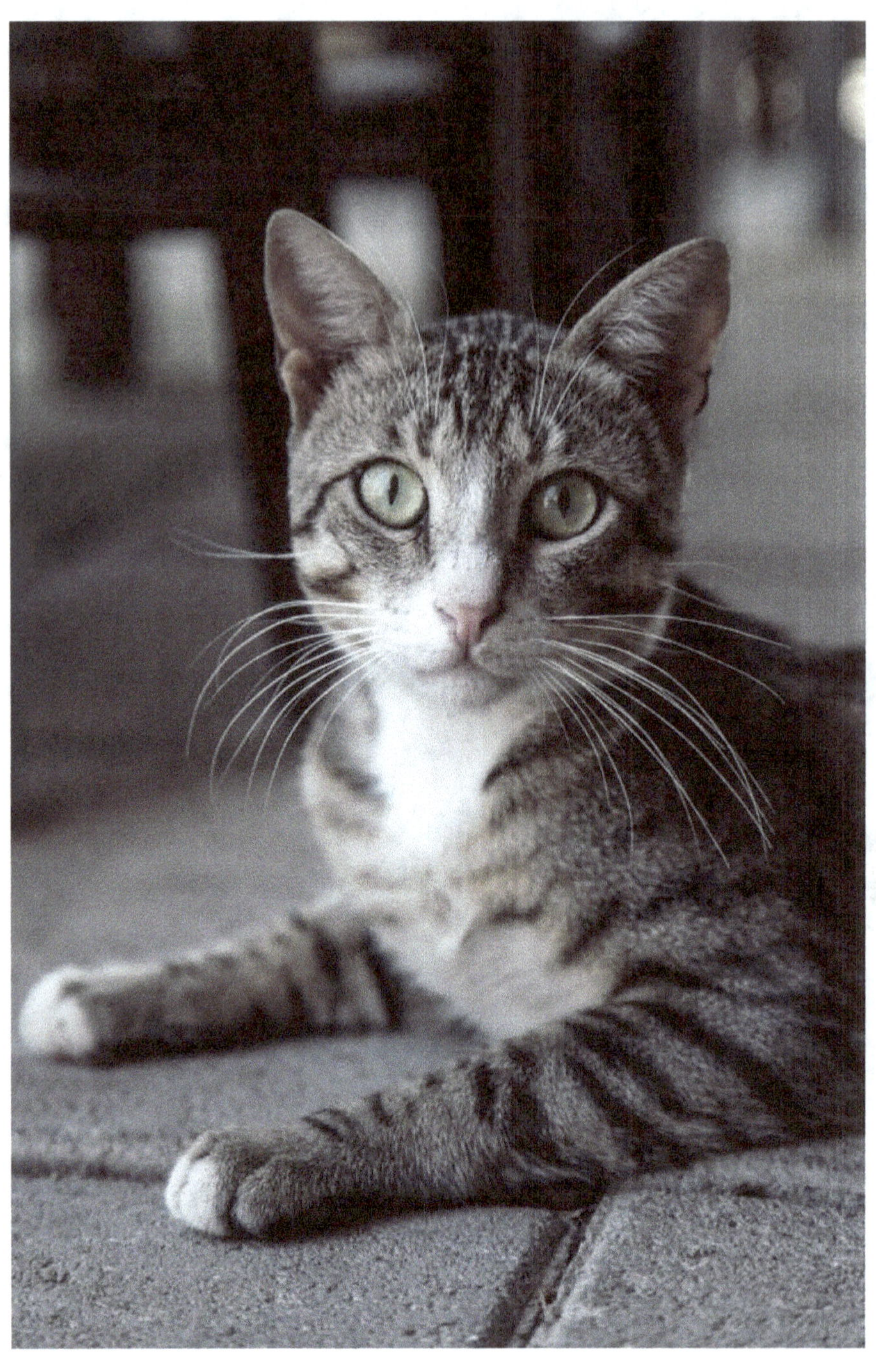

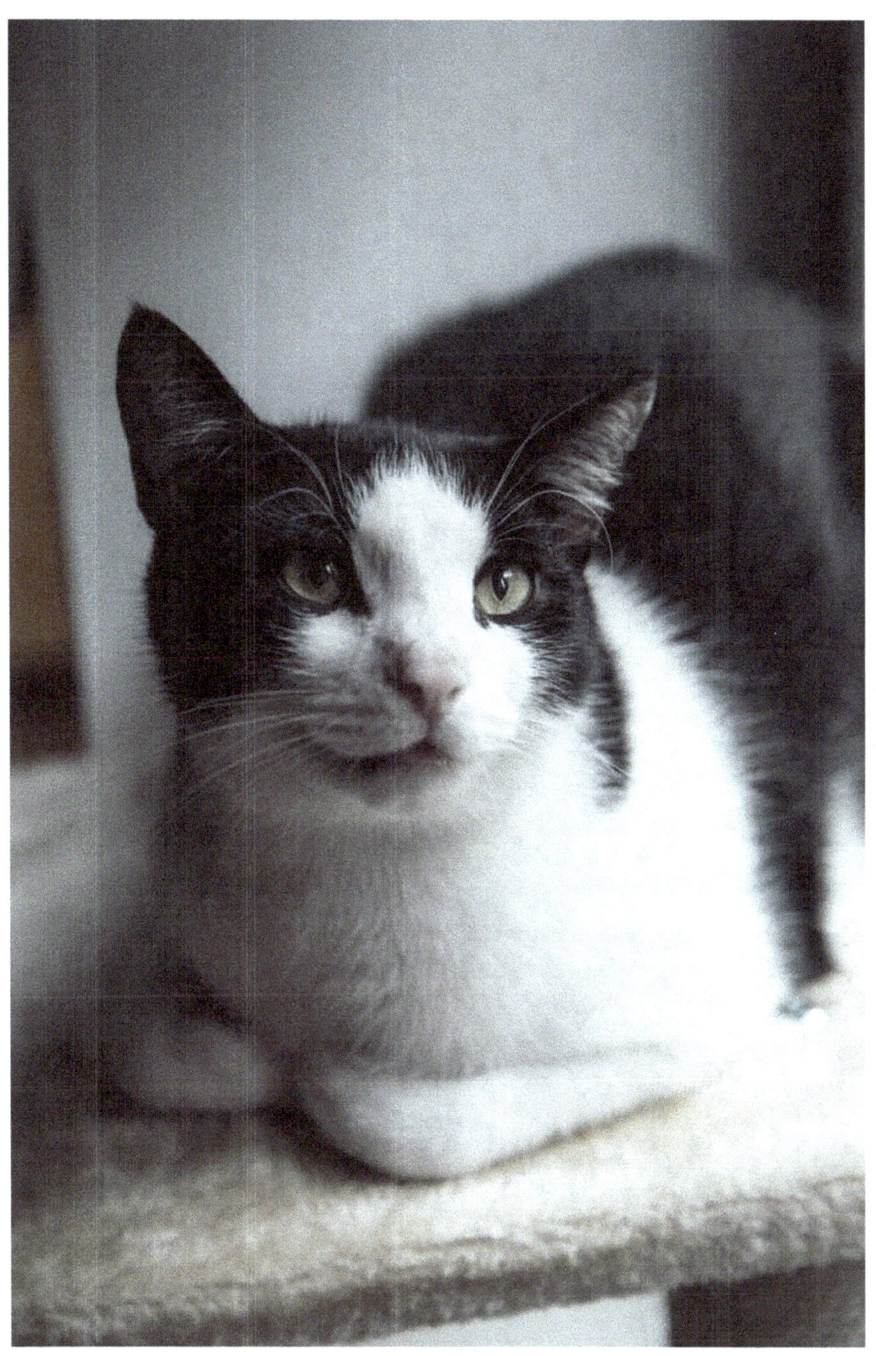

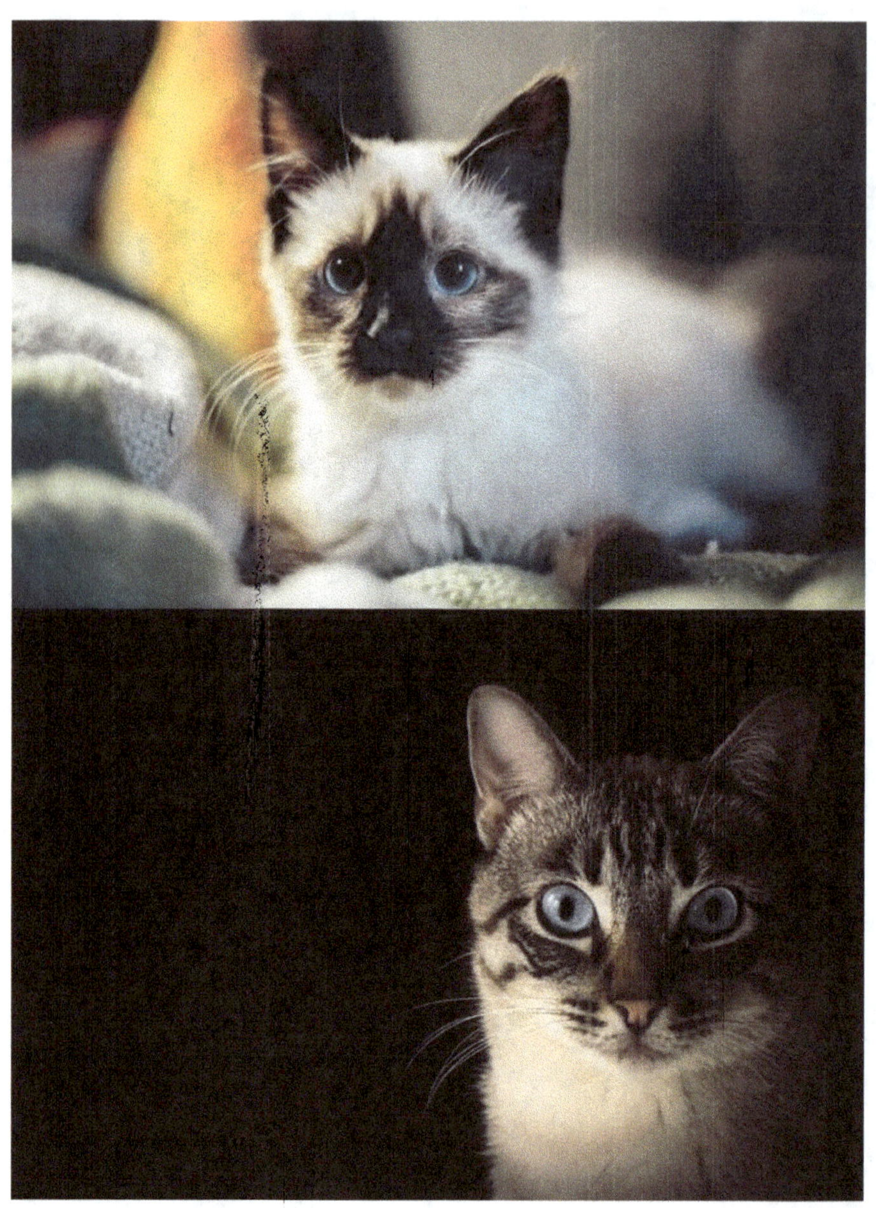

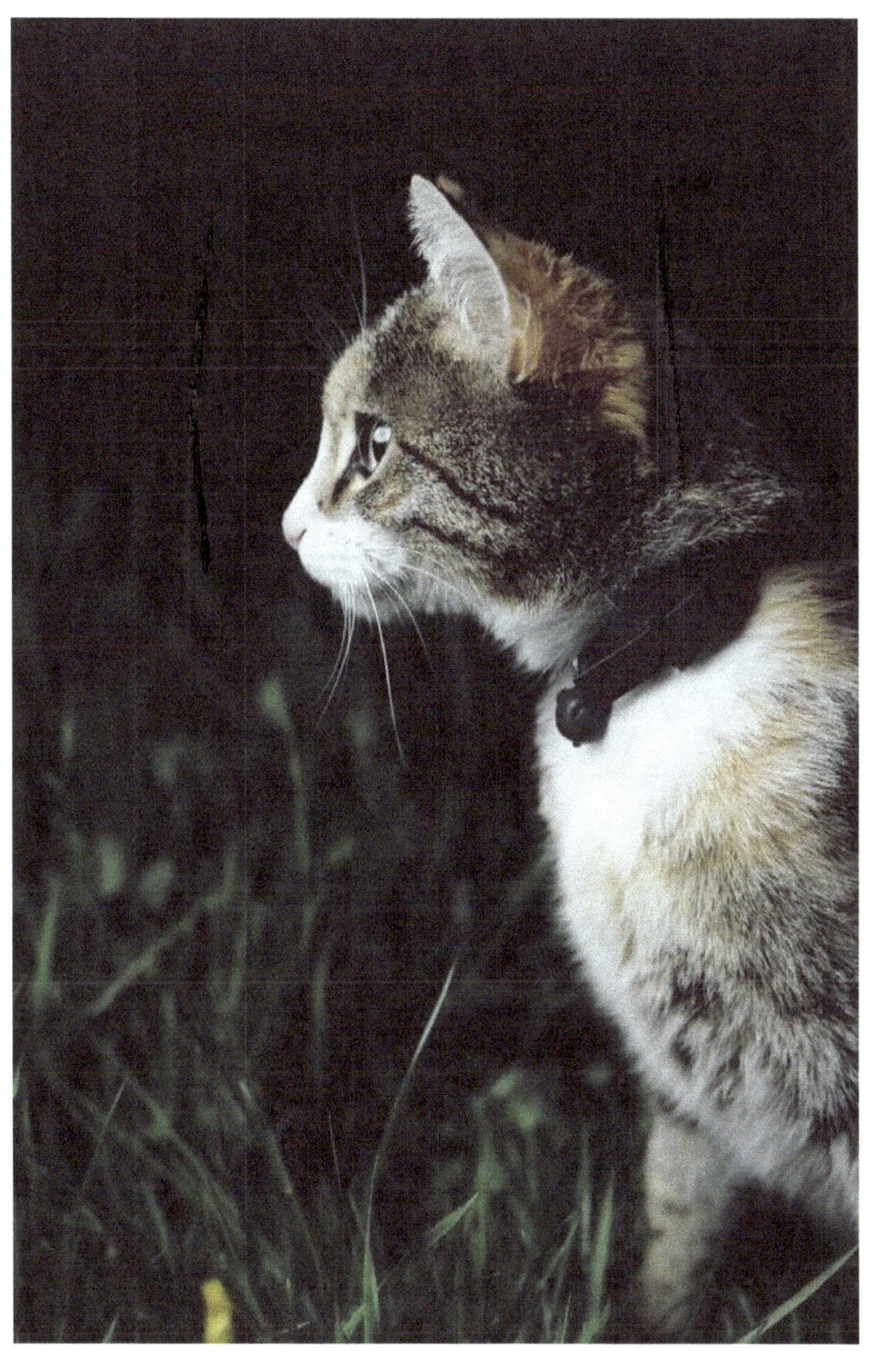

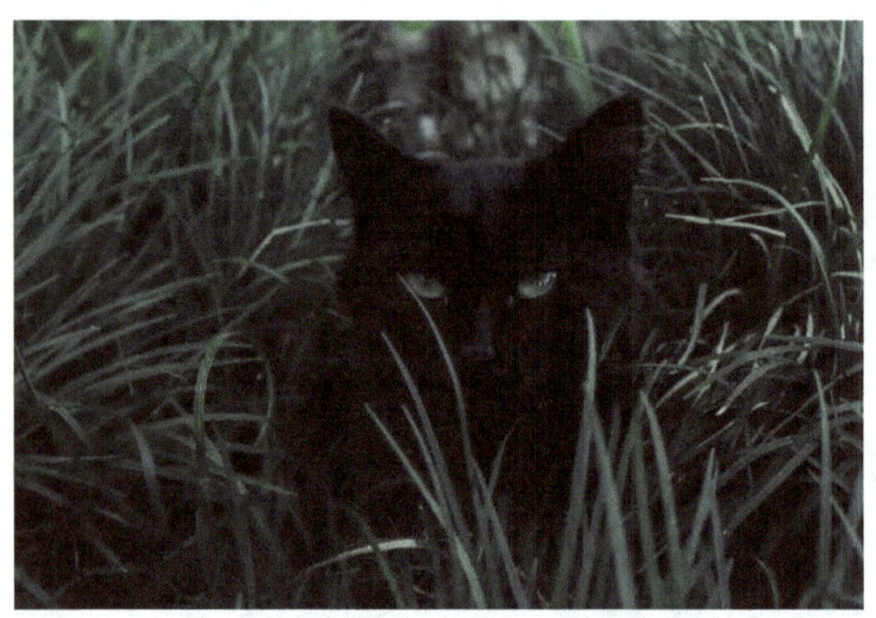

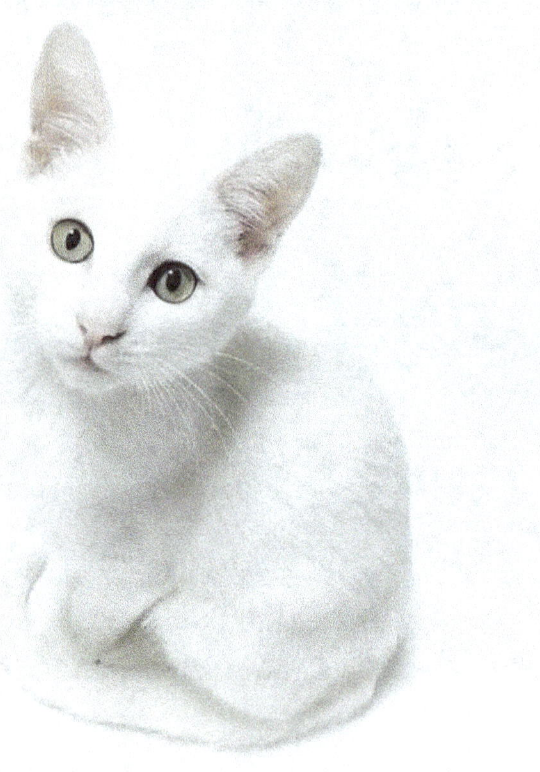

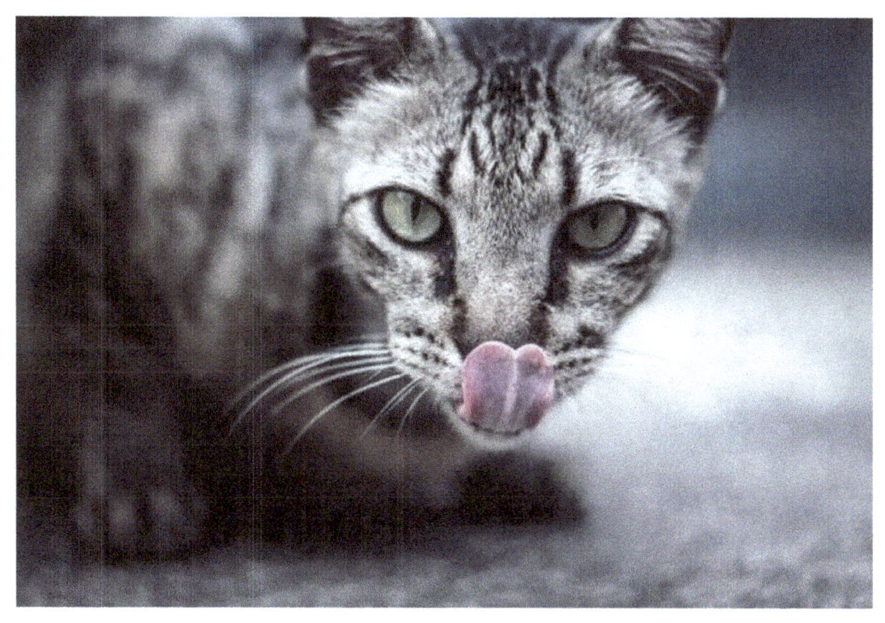

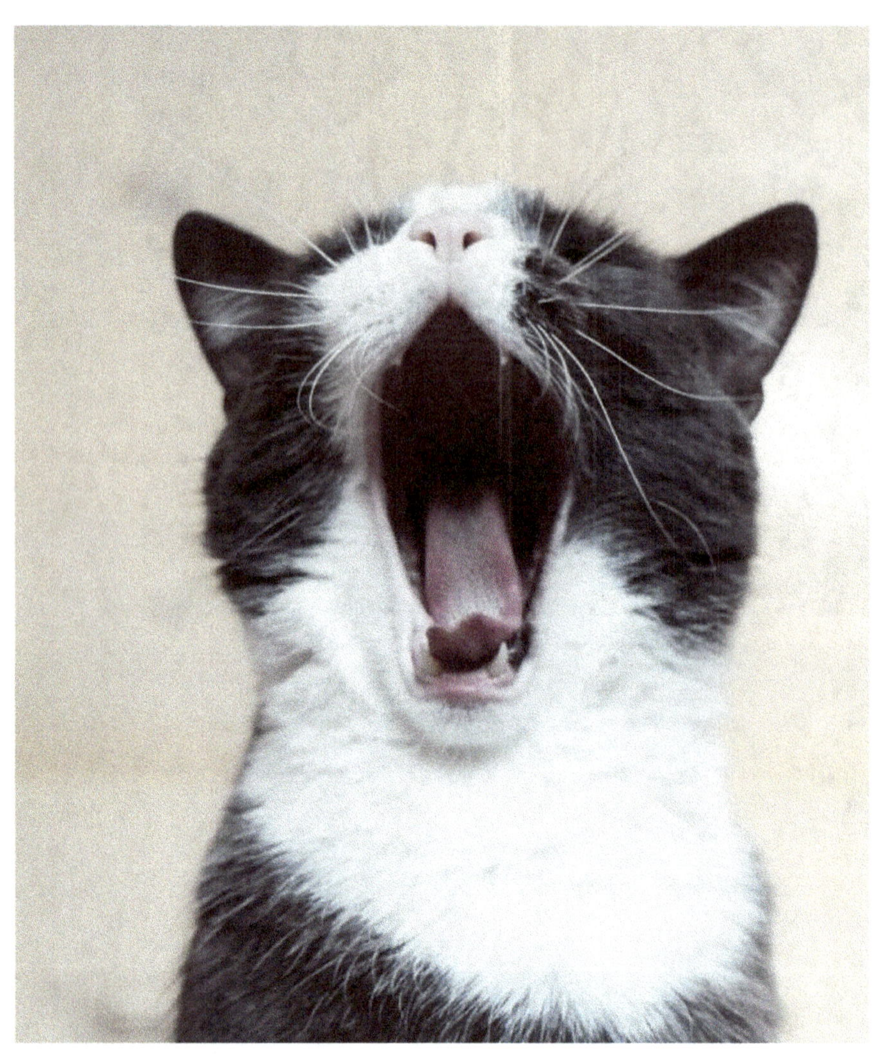

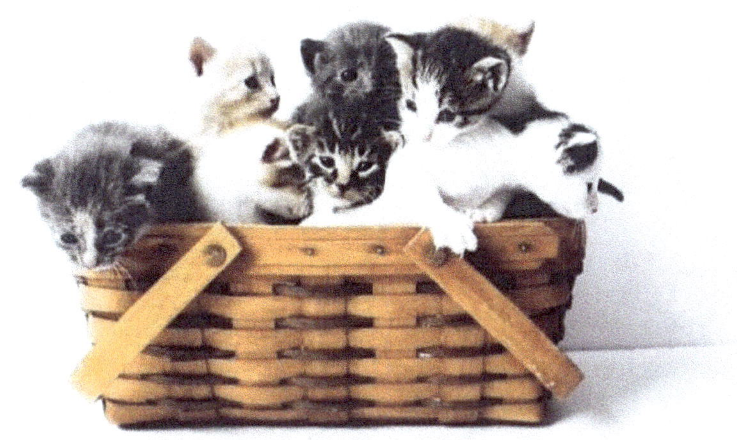

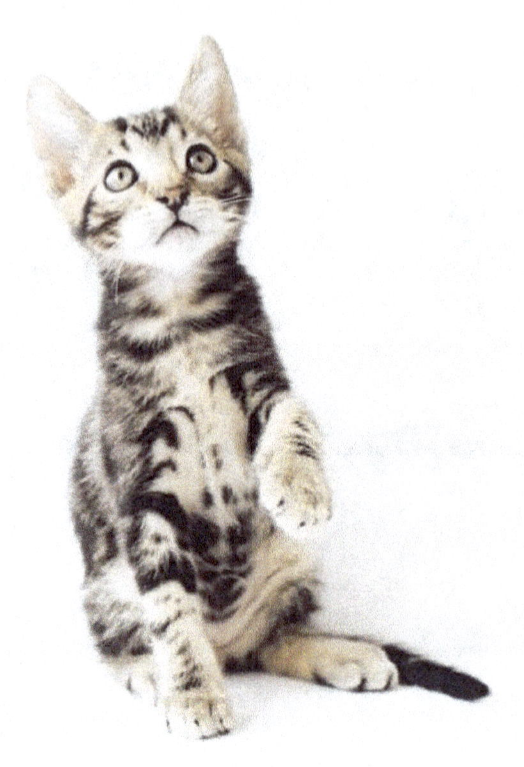

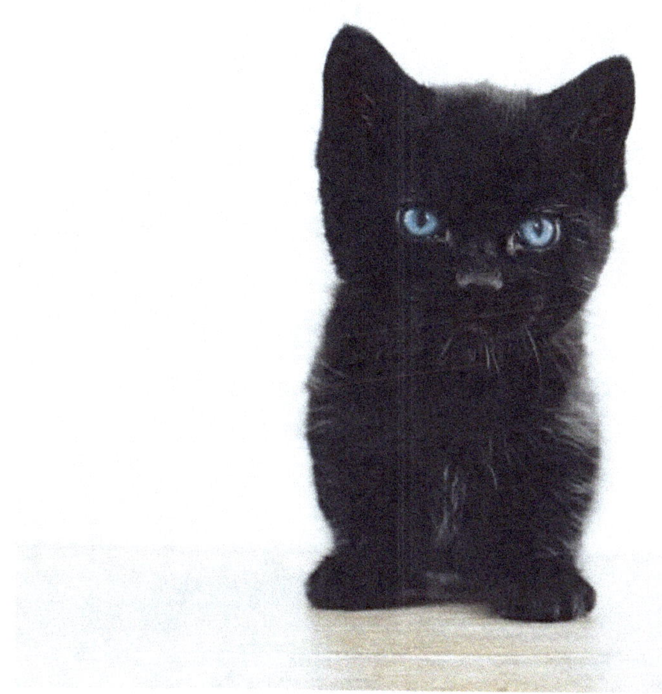

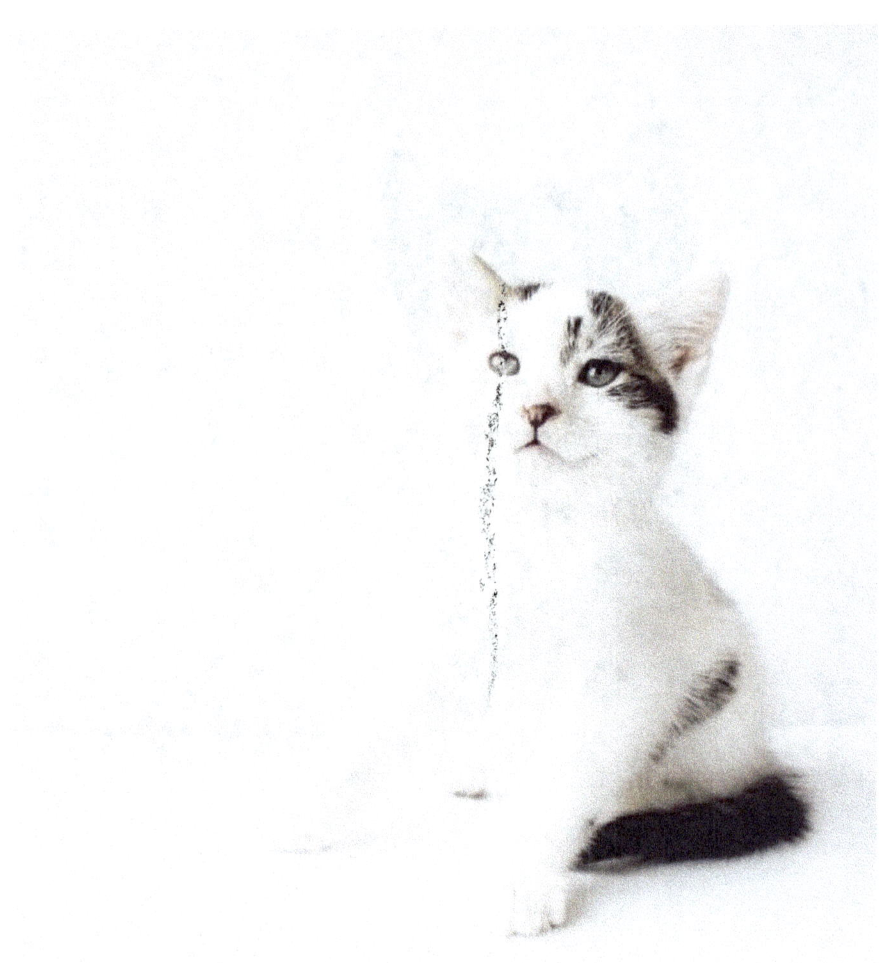

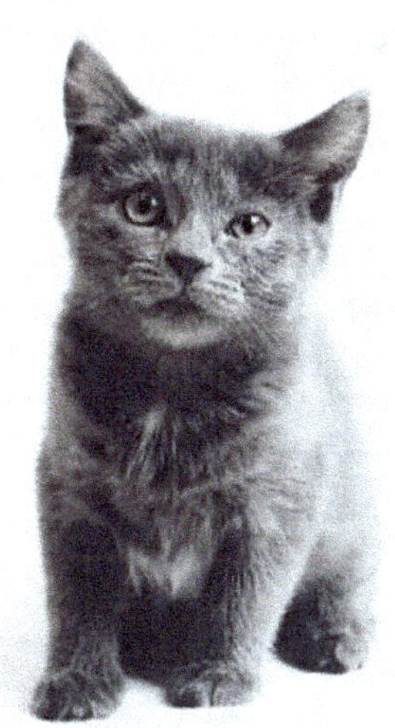

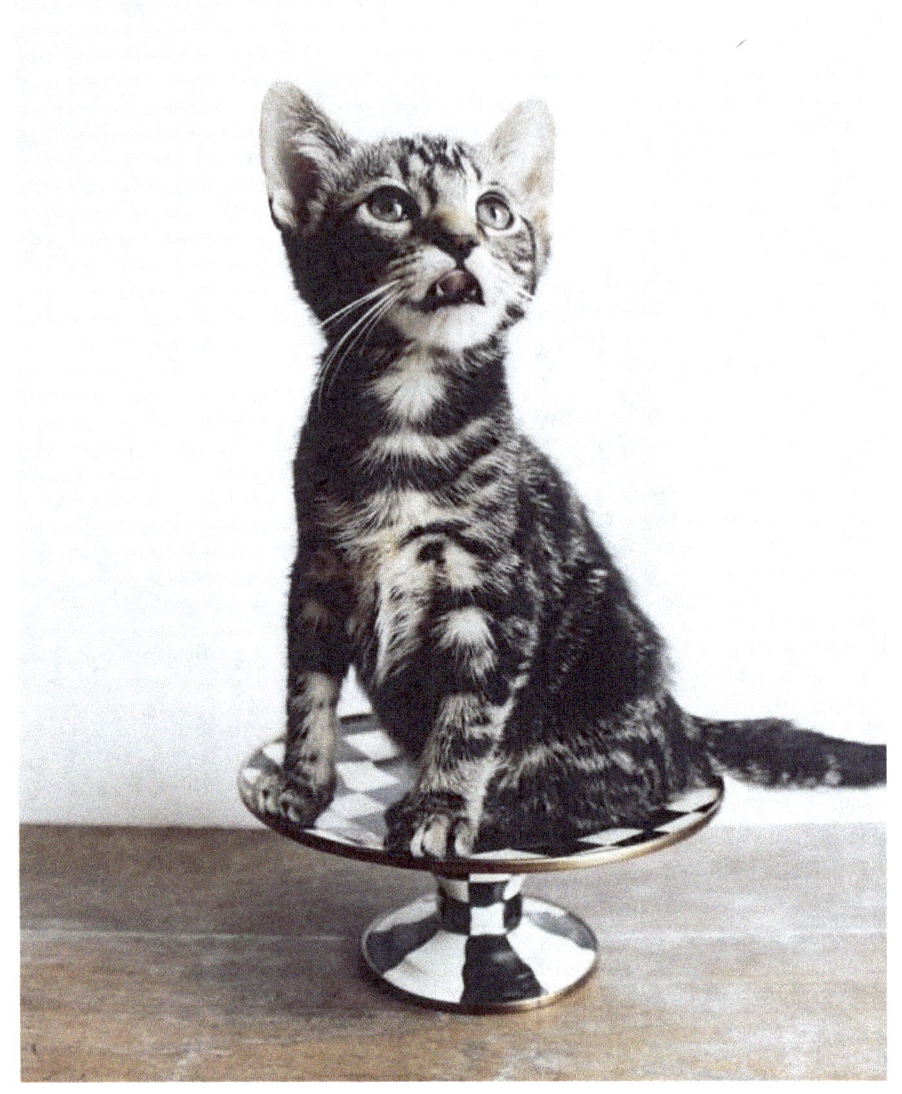

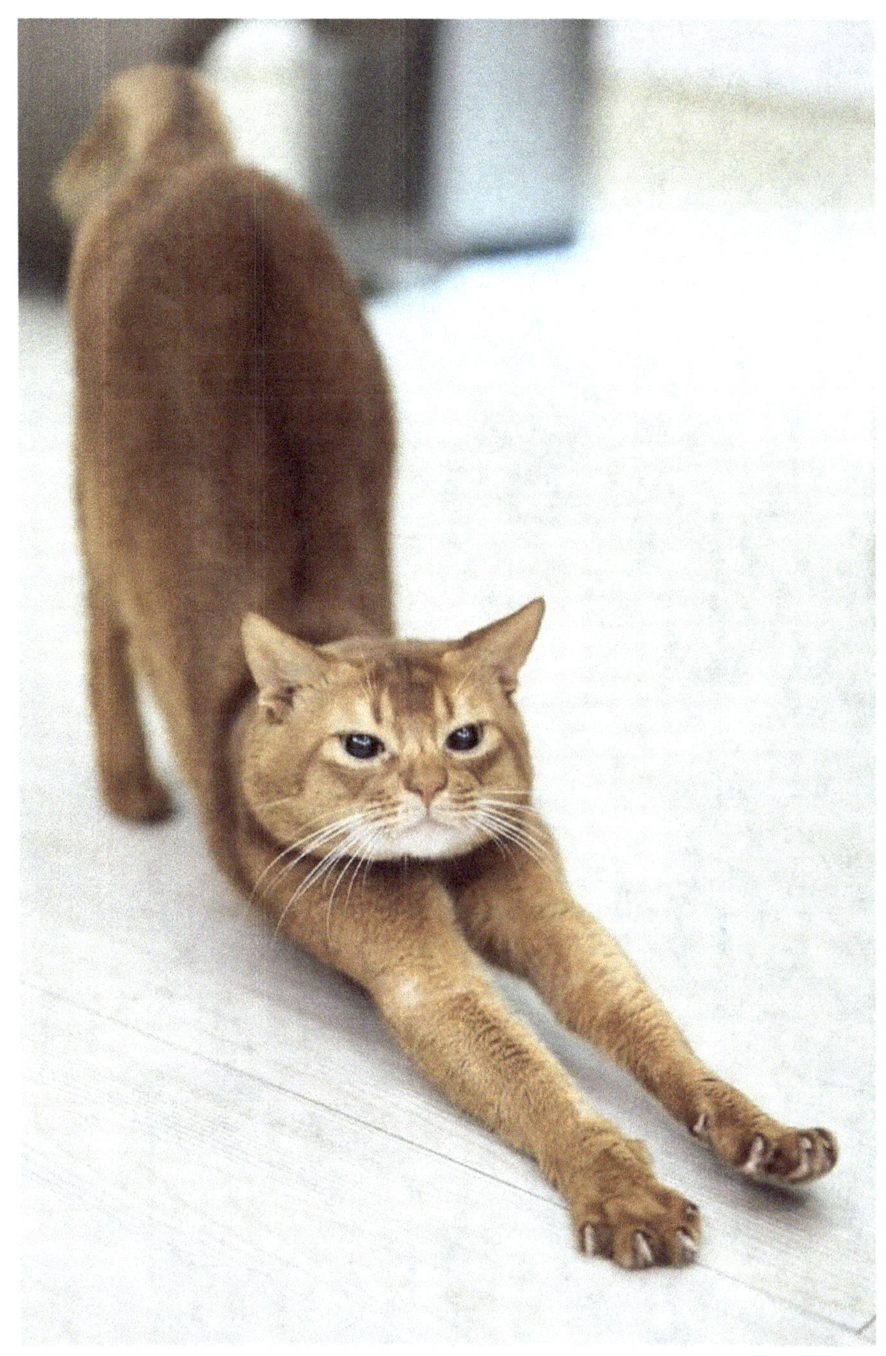

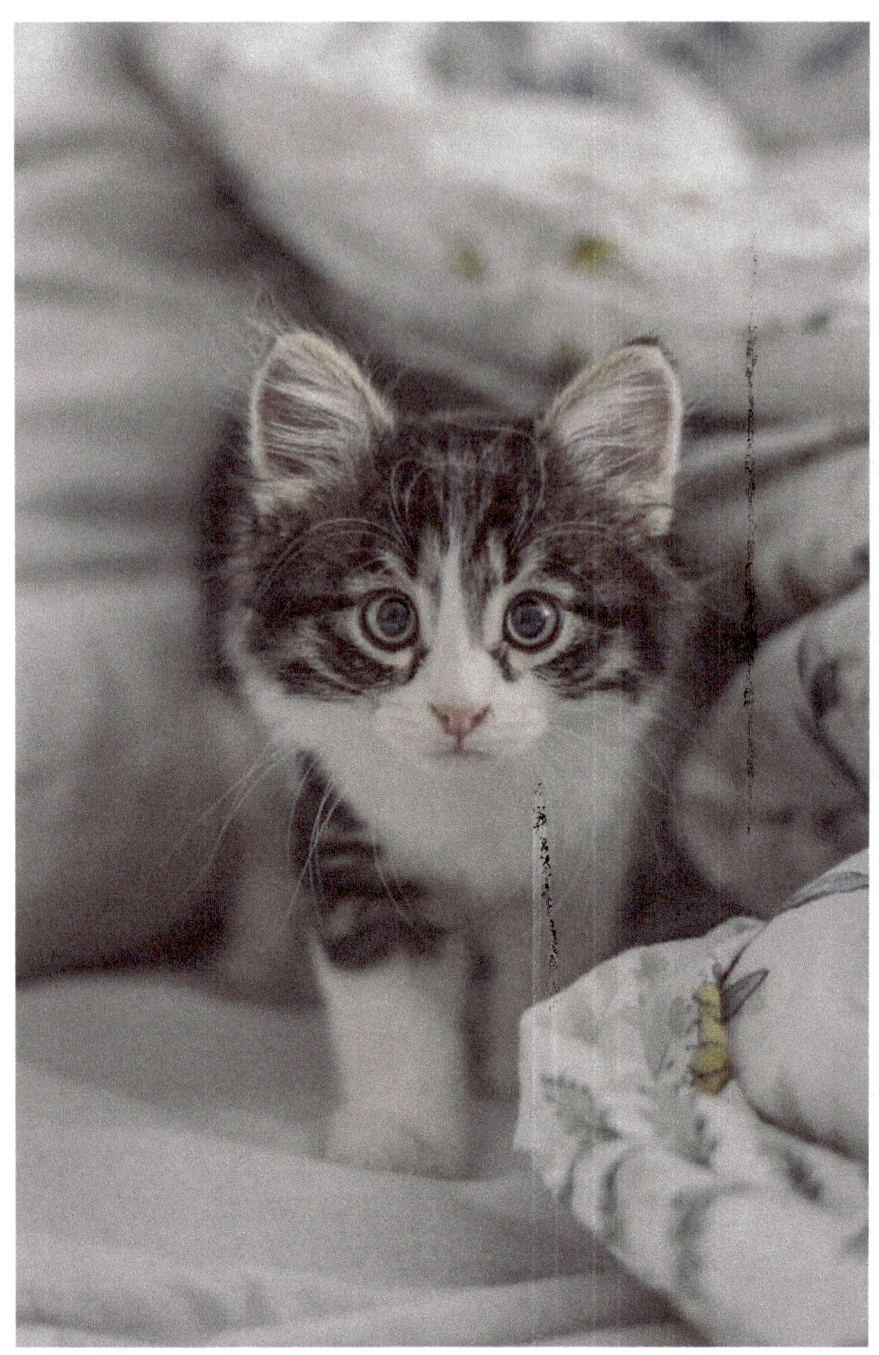

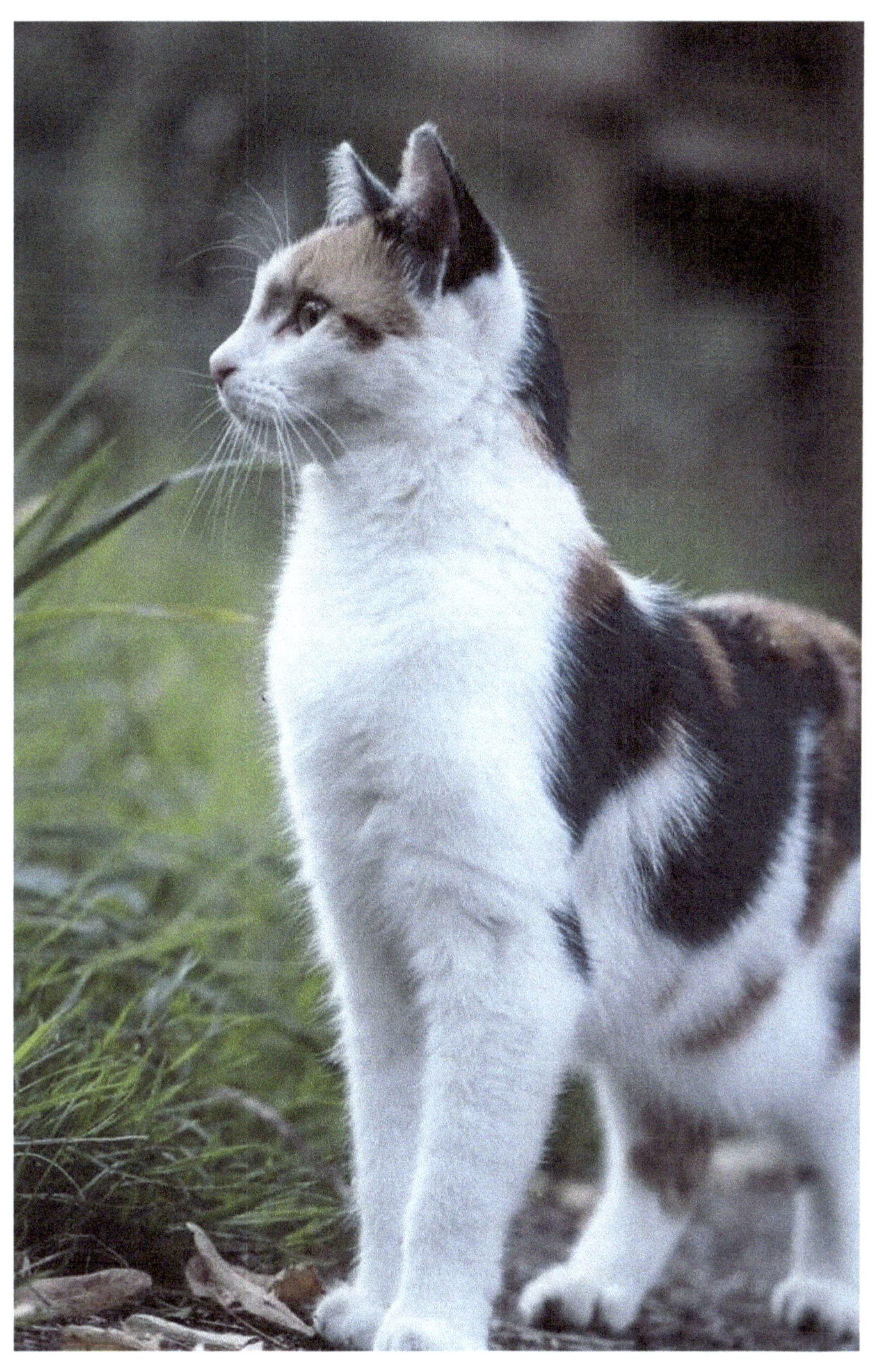

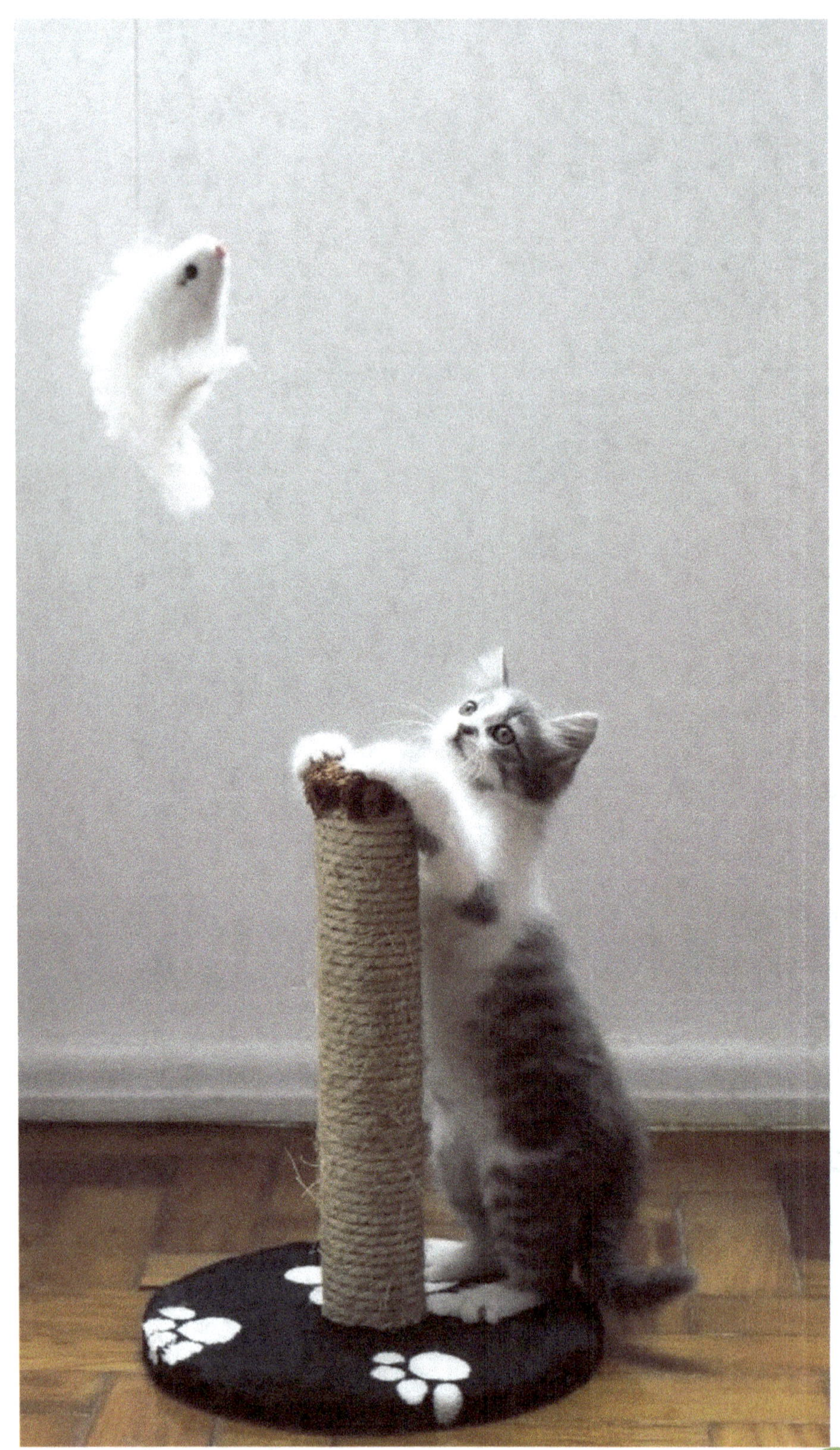

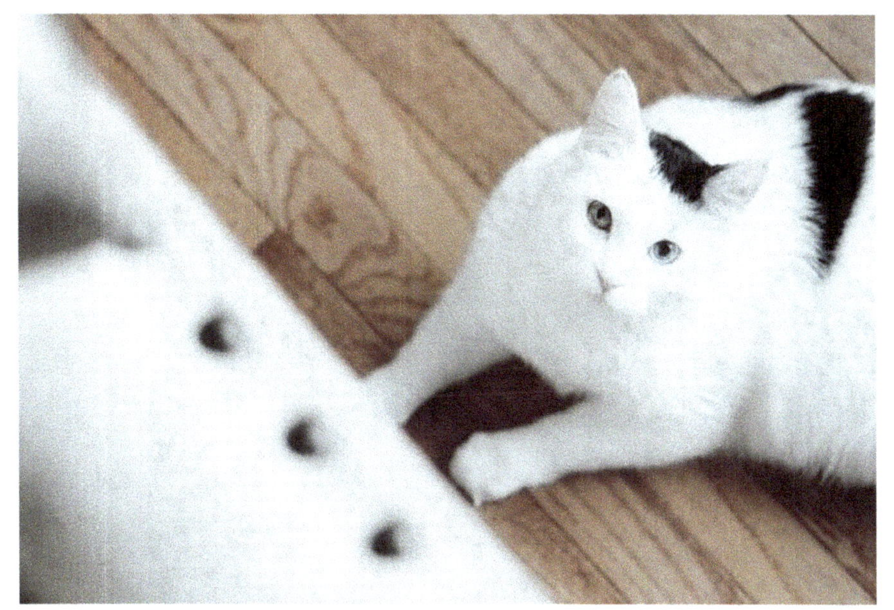

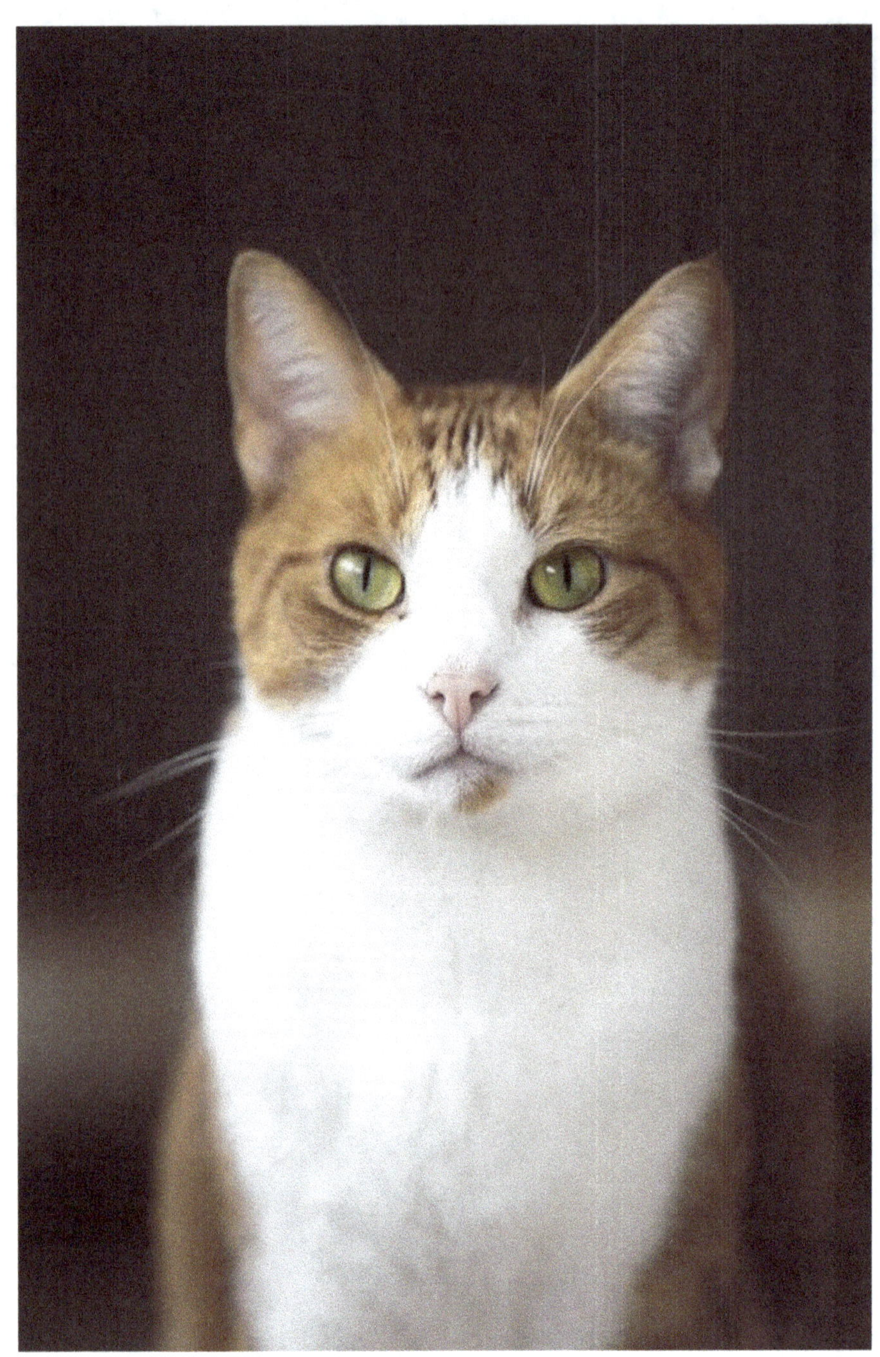

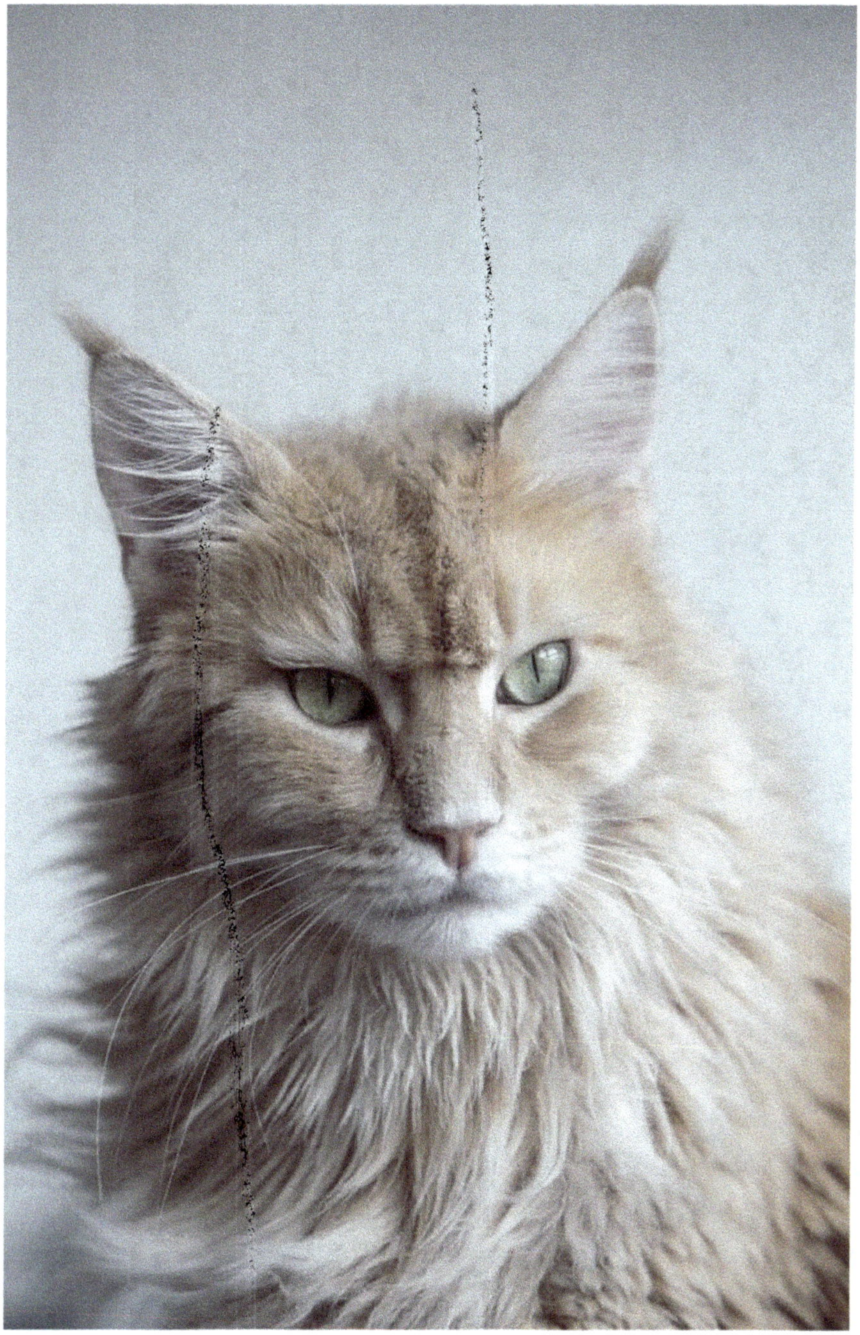

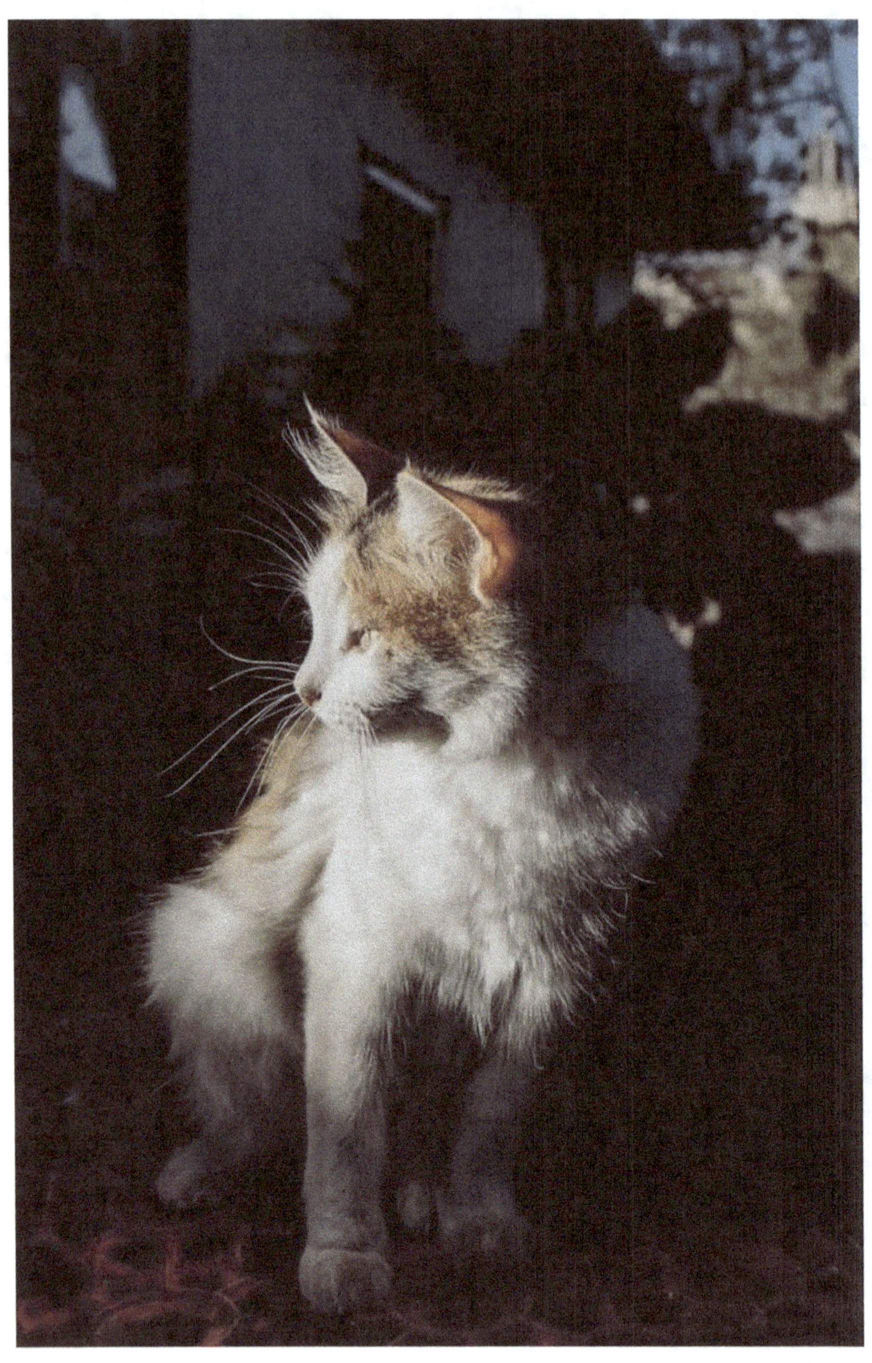

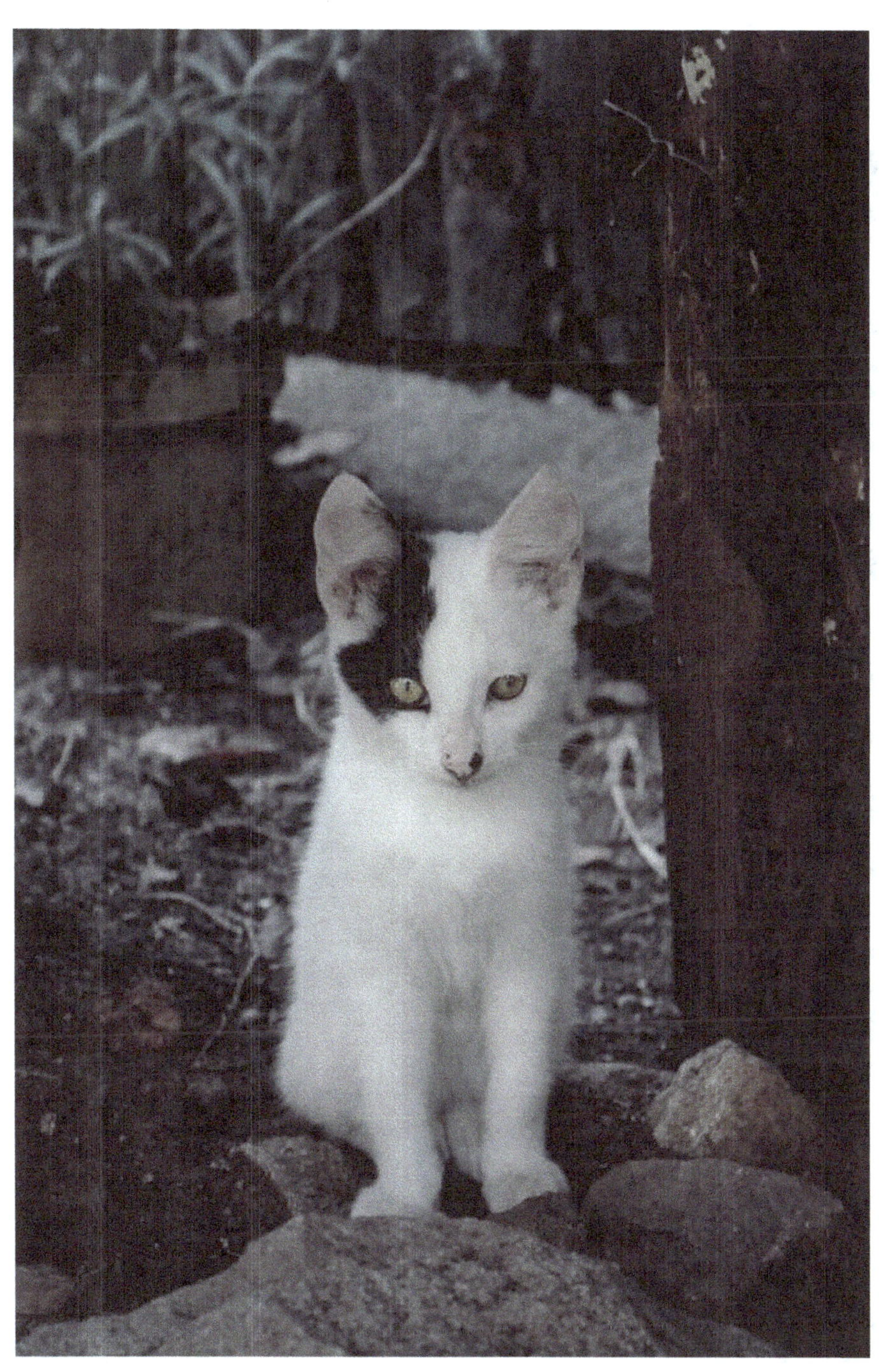

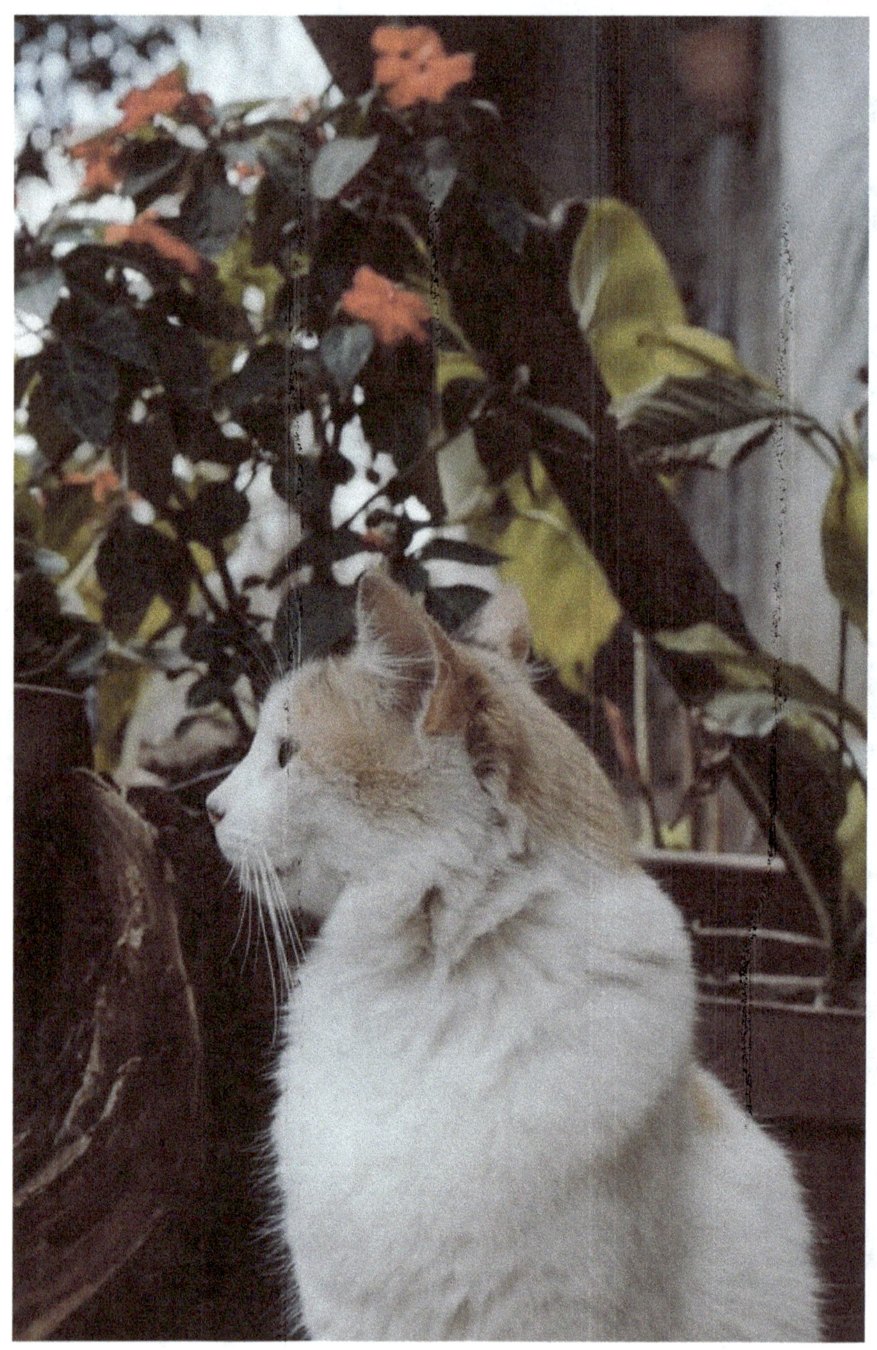

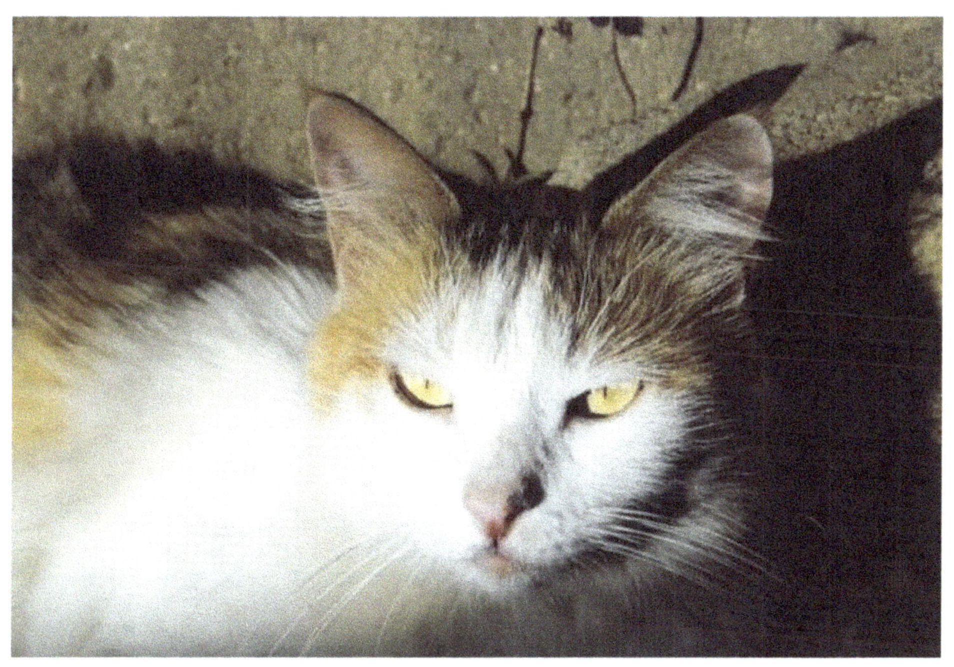

"Cats are inquisitive, but hate to admit it." – Mason Cooley